PROPERTY SUCCESS MINDSET

PAUL MCFADDEN

Copyright © 2020 by Paul McFadden

All rights reserved.

Published by TMD Media Ltd 2020

ISBN: 9798655125353
Revision: 24/Jul/2020

ALL RIGHTS RESERVED

No part of this publication may be reproduced, stored in or introduced into a retrieval system, or transmitted, in any form, or by any means (electronic, mechanical, photocopying, recording, or otherwise) without the prior written permission of the publisher. This book is sold subject to the condition that it shall not, by way of trade or otherwise, be lent, resold, hired out, or otherwise circulated without the publisher's prior written consent in any form of binding or cover other than that in which it is published and without a similar condition including this condition being imposed on the subsequent purchaser.

EDITORIAL TEAM

Billy Farrell, Aislinn Stumpf, Sean McIntyre, Dylan Stewart, and Richard Swan.

BOOK COVER DESIGN

TMD Media Ltd and Rose Chanel Art

PUBLISHER'S DISCLAIMER

Readers of this publication agree that neither Paul McFadden, Paul McFadden Wealth Ltd, nor the publisher will be held responsible or liable for damages that may be alleged as resulting directly or indirectly from the use of this publication. Neither the publisher nor the author can be held accountable for the information provided by, or actions resulting from, accessing these resources.

DEDICATION

This book is dedicated to my clients, who go to work each day to progress, expand and evolve; both personally and professionally.

Nothing pleases me more than to see your growth and the accompanying results across each area of life over time.

You are what drives me.

You are what matters most.

Your success is everything.

I wrote this book as a companion for you.

To all past, present, and future clients, I salute you.

ACKNOWLEDGEMENTS

First and foremost, I would like to thank my beautiful wife Alexna, and my children, Arya and Hannah, for their unending support, inspiration, and love.

I would like to thank the entire team at PMW and TMD Media for their relentless commitment to push the boundaries, for their commitment to changing lives, and for their support in doing what we do. I'm proud to be a part of this family. I would also like to thank Dylan Stewart, Sean McIntyre, and Richard Swan for their editorial contributions and support.

My greatest thanks in writing this book are to Billy Farrell and Aislinn Stumpf, whose dedication and efforts have been exceptional. It's been my privilege and honour to work with you.

CONTENTS

Introduction	i
What Do You Want?	1
Reprogramming For Wealth	9
What Stops You?	27
Pandemics, Recessions and Acts of God	35
The Good Opinion of Other People	45
Finding the Belief and Confidence	55
Finding the Money	65
Finding the Deals	75
Finding the Time	85
Finding the Right Information and Support	93
Moving Forward: The War Plan	105
Next Steps: Property Protege ®	115
About the Author	125

PROPERTY SUCCESS MINDSET

INTRODUCTION

Is it possible to generate substantial cash flow through Property?

Is it possible to create financial freedom through Property?

Is it possible to build serious wealth through Property?

We all know the answers to these questions. After all, this *is* Property we're talking about. These results, and more, are all very possible. Now let's change it up a little. Is it possible to achieve these things *fast*? Is it possible to *get rich quick*?

When my eyes first turned towards making money, it was with a *get rich quick* Mindset. I would sit at home on my PC, complete with 56k dial-up modem, in a flat I shared with my mum and sisters, searching online for ways to *get rich*, and *quick*.

Is it any wonder then, that I *didn't* get rich? It wasn't for the lack of trying. I worked hard, but later realised I was focused on all the wrong things. I went in with a me-focus. I wasn't interested in creating value. I wasn't considering the bigger picture.

The drive for change was understandable. My living environment was difficult. I grew in a tough housing estate on Glasgows Southside, deep in a culture of drink drugs and gangs. The topic of money was taboo. The general attitude towards money and those who had it was negative. I was tired of it. I wanted change. I watched the world go by and wondered why *we* struggled to get by, whilst others thrived. I wanted out. I wanted more of what life had to offer. I wanted my shot.

And so, I searched for ways to make it happen. What I didn't realise at the time, was that I, Paul McFadden, was merely replicating the actions and errors of the many other misguided or misinformed people who'd tried and failed in the pursuit of 'better.'

Why? Because I was *doing* it all wrong, which ultimately stemmed from a Mindset which ran at the polar opposite end of the scale of what was required to build and retain wealth. My Mindset was poor. Subsequently, so too, were my results.

Here's a little secret for you. When your focus is *get rich quick*, it's most likely you *won't* get rich. But when your focus is fixed on building something to last, with patience, over time; then there's a high chance you could get rich, whatever *rich* means to you, and it *doesn't* have to take forever.

This is a book like no other. There will be no talk or illusion of overnight success or quick millions. If that's what you're hoping for, you've picked up the wrong book. More to the point, there is no book that can help you with that.

However, if you feel the continual magnetic pull towards creating a life that makes you feel you're *truly* living, that ticks all the right boxes based on what *you* want more of; if you feel or know that Property is the key to making it possible; and if you're prepared and ready to do what it's going to take for that to happen, then read on.

THERE ARE MANY REASONS PEOPLE DON'T MAKE IT

They allow the opinions of others to stop them. They are paralysed by limiting beliefs. They don't have the time. They get the wrong information. They don't have the support. They don't take appropriate action. They make costly mistakes. They allow fear to dominate them. They lack the motivation. They never build the momentum. They don't know how to find the money. They don't know where to find the deals.

And let's not forget Global Pandemics.

The list goes on. But the underlying cause is always the same. It all comes down to Mindset, our Mental game of Property. It's *not* about what happens to you. It's about what you choose to do with what happens. It's *not* about resources. It's about resourcefulness. It's *not* about what's possible or not. It's about raising your inner game.

After all, if others have done it, why not you? I made it happen. Hundreds upon hundreds of people who've come through our Property Protege ® Programme have made it happen. Hundreds of thousands of others across the UK, the US, and worldwide, have made it happen. So why not you?

It's important to remember, that 'if a thing is humanly possible, and has been achieved by many other people, then it's within reach.' For example, there are 46.8 Million Millionaires in the world at the time of writing. If becoming a Millionaire is your goal, then I ask again, why not you? What's stopping you? Because if nothing was stopping you, you'd be there already, or at the very least, well on your way.

It's all rhetorical of course. The reality is, if you want it, and it's possible, then get after it. But first, to allow that to happen, let's work on what matters most, and what makes everything else possible.

MINDSET IS EVERYTHING

When I went to Dan "The Trillion Dollar Man" Pena's castle for 10 days, the first few days were focused on Mindset. When people join our Property Protege Programme, the first six hours of the live event are focused on Mindset. Some people, however, just want to know how to *do the deals,* and how to *find the money.* What matters significantly *more,* is *becoming the kind of person* who can do the deals, and *becoming the kind of person* worth funding, partnering with, or investing in.

Economies change. Industries change. Markets change. Rules change. Things change. The one constant we can always rely on, is change. What can never be changed or altered by any third party, however, is the Mindset of a champion. It's not in what you do. It's always, first, in who you become.

Let's say you put Richard Branson on an alternate planet earth. No contacts. No resources. No money. What do you think would happen within a relatively short space of time? Would he dwindle in idleness? Or would he begin to create?

Flip the coin for a moment. Do you know what happens to most lottery winners? Statistically, north of 60% of those who win the lottery go broke within 2 years of winning. In fact, if you ever find yourself with a Million pounds, you'd best *quickly* become a Millionaire. Let that one sink in for a moment.

HOME TRUTHS AND LESSONS LEARNED

If I were to list *all* the things I did wrong in the early days, we'd be here forever. What I will do, is weave the most important mistakes and failures I've personally gone through into this book as lesson points, to help you avoid the same. I've made every mistake imaginable. I didn't have guidance, support, or mentorship in the early days. I didn't see the value in investing in my education. You've purchased this book, which puts you way ahead of me when I first started. Well done, for that.

I've had failed attempts in business. I've found myself in terrible debt. I've chosen the wrong partners. I've been misled. I've built portfolios with consortiums only to be thrown aside with no protection. I built my portfolio from 2009 entirely in my own name, without taking tax or other implications into account. My first deal almost took me out of the game. It took years of trading before I stopped being irresponsible around the money I was making and began to set up company structures. I've had every fear, every excuse, every reason for procrastination and giving up. I've been naive. I've been foolish. I've felt painfully alone in some very dark places. I've made money, and lost it. I've made friends, and lost them. You name it, I've been there and gone through it.

That, was the first part of my journey. It was, shall we say, a learning experience. There were good points and lots of wins in there, but for the most part, let's just say I learned a lot. So why would you take advice from me, with *that* track record? Let's fast forward to the second part of the journey.

From a fairly hopeless start, I then went on to buy and flip millions of pounds worth of Property. I've packaged and traded tens of millions of pounds worth of Property deals to other investors. I've been responsible for helping countless others get started, including many prominent and well-known people in the industry, and have built a substantial seven-figure personal portfolio. My focus is split across multiple investments, developments, projects and businesses, which I own and control, minus the ego boost of having to have my name on them. Don't get me wrong, bad things can still happen. They still do and always will. That's business. The trajectory, however, over the past eight or nine years, despite fluctuations, has continually been an upward trend.

My life is very different today, from the life of the 20 year old living in his mums flat, searching for ways and means of creating wealth. I live between my primary residence in Gleneagles in Scotland, London, and our home in Costa Rica. I've had every car and toy that most people only dream of. I spend most of my time travelling. I've created a level of financial freedom and abundance that could sustain my family for several lifetimes. I work with phenomenal individuals and have a great team around me. Looking past the monetary and physical aspects, my absolute priority in life is my beautiful wife Alexna, and our two young daughters, Arya and Hannah. I don't say any of this to impress you. I say it to impress upon you, that if I can achieve what I would consider success through Property, and if the people who've come through our Property Protege Programme can each achieve their subjective ideas of success in Property, and if many others in the industry can do the same, then you, the person reading this now, can do it too.

It's not going to be easy. There will be challenges. It won't happen overnight. But, once you get your Mindset in check, as I had to, you'll realise it's much more possible than you may have initially thought. And the best part? It doesn't have to take anywhere near as long as it took me. Learn from my mistakes. Learn from my wins. Learn from this book. The gap between where you are and where you want to be is internal. It happens internally before it happens externally. This book will bridge that gap.

READY TO CHART A NEW COURSE?

I have a deep passion for what I do. I have an equal passion for supporting others in doing the same. I'm also well aware that in an unregulated training industry, people don't always get the best advice. Sometimes this results in failed attempts that dampen the hopes and dreams of the aspiring Property investor. Sometimes people bow out entirely, becoming cynical or washing their hands of the idea. Sometimes people are led into serious debt, or down the garden path, and worse.

My goal is to help you understand what's possible, what it's really going to take, and who you'll have to become to get there. There will be no sugarcoating or softening. There will be no punches pulled. There will be no high fives, back slaps, or dancing. I'll speak directly. I'll be blunt. You might not always like what I have to say. That's ok. My job is to help you get your number one asset in the *right* place. My job is to help you win.

By the end of the book, providing you've given it your full attention, you'll have the foundations in place to aggressively move forward on your Property journey, regardless of where you're starting from or your own circumstances. Throughout, you'll come to realise that the majority of things that hold people back, are nothing more than constructs in our own minds, and if we can get past them, whilst re-channeling our focus, we open up to a whole new world of possibility. We're about to go on a journey, that makes what you may have considered to be 'an impossible game,' entirely possible.

Make this book your constant companion in Property. Continually refer to it. Challenge the ideas. Share it with others. Underline text. Highlight paragraphs. Argue with it. Wear it out through continual use. My point; make sure you make use of it.

CHAPTER 1:
WHAT DO YOU WANT?

This book is not necessarily about becoming a millionaire, nor achieving financial freedom, building wealth, or creating cash flow. Not as such. Rather, it's about becoming the kind of person who *can*. It's about the mental building blocks required to successfully achieve what you want in life.

Which begs the question. What *do* you want? Why *are* you reading this book? Of course, there are a variety of reasons why someone would desire an increased quality of life with Property as their chosen vehicle, but why are *you* here? What do *you* want? Is it to supplement your pension? To enjoy the finer things? To travel the world? To create security? To achieve peace of mind and a sense of freedom? To provide a comfort blanket for future generations? What is it you want?

PROPERTY IS THE PATH

Very rarely, if ever, do people get started in Property for the love of bricks and mortar. Property is a vehicle. It's a means to an end. It's an industry in which you can leverage a variety of strategies in order to profit. It's rarely about Property; it's about the end result.

Many people reading this will have attempted other ventures at various points, and may still be venturing. Some will have tried various things and failed. Some will be disheartened. Some will have achieved a low level, or in rare cases, a substantial level, of success. Typical approaches and vehicles include Forex, Cryptocurrency, drop-shipping, affiliate marketing, and network marketing.

What most fail to realise, however, is that the problem is rarely the opportunity itself, rather, it's the Mindset and subsequent actions of the individual. If you've tried various things and failed, understand that it's most likely not the thing itself. More often than not, the problem, is you. And whatever you move onto next, you're taking the biggest blockage along for the ride. This isn't something to become disheartened over. It's something to become aware of in order to change.

And then there are those who set out to start a business. They've bought into the entrepreneurial dream, perhaps after watching shows such as Dragons Den or The Apprentice, or having a bright idea of their own. Of course, without realising the substantial personal sacrifice required to make it a reality. A typical business owner-operator, for example, carries the weight and responsibility of every element of their business. They employ a team of professionals to bear the load of each moving part, but the ultimate responsibility and liability of the enterprise lands at their own door. And whether the business scales, or conversely, struggles to grow, cash flow is an ever-present factor. Many business owners find themselves working harder than they would in a job, for minimal upside, and many would be better off in employment.

The majority of truly successful entrepreneurs *(who also happen to be in the minority of those who've been given - or have given themselves - the title)*, generally do not achieve wealth through the daily grind. They achieve their wealth by owning various profitable enterprises. They strike deals. They buy, turnaround and sell. They invest. They flip. They are by-and-large, transactional in their approach.

I love business. However, I learned a long time ago, that there was a monumental difference between what it means to work *in* a given business, and to work *on* it.

Property is the means to your end. There are other opportunities available, many of which can be lucrative, but none so much as Property, in my humble opinion, and more importantly, in my experience. Property can allow you to create substantial wealth. It can allow you to generate predictable and ever-increasing cash flow. It can give you the opportunity to create the lifestyle you desire. And at its very core, Property is a transactional business, allowing for big wins on a semi-regular basis. It is the ultimate vehicle for financial success.

SO WHAT DO YOU WANT?

Success is an entirely subjective experience; different from one person to the next. For some, success is monetary; for others, it's all encompassing. For some, success is security; for others, it's freedom. We all want different things, and in varying degrees. Success, therefore, is a personal affair. So an important question to ask yourself, is *what does success look like to you?*

Anything is possible through Property, but we must approach the entire journey like there are no limits to our abilities, and then sensibly begin to build at pace. And if anything is possible, then you can have what you want, whatever that is for you. A bold statement for sure, but one rooted in fact. As we've already established, this is Property. With the right Mindset, knowledge, strategy and action, even those from the most challenging of circumstances, can enjoy an enhanced quality of life and more of what they want, as has been proven time and time again.

As we've discussed, if a thing is humanly possible, and has been achieved by many others, then why not for you too? And yet, despite this reality, most people generally don't set goals for what they truly want in a way that lights them up and inspires action. Perhaps a few New Years resolutions slip in at the end of December, but just as easily and a little more quietly slip out a day or two *into* January. Some people do set larger goals, but when they don't achieve them, it can cause them to scale back, lower their standards in terms of what they want, and make their outcomes more realistic, shall we say. Perhaps they do shoot for the same target again, but this time, making a few less people aware of it. And then there are those who do set and achieve larger goals. I can tell you one thing for sure, it wasn't through hope or luck.

I regularly set, drive toward, and achieve big goals. When setting my goals, I'm like a kid at Christmas, writing my letter to Santa, and placing it under the tree, detailing what I *want*, not what society has conditioned me to expect. Goals should be big enough that they scare you. They should be bold enough that people laugh at you. They should be exciting enough that the very pursuit of them makes you feel alive. And the timeline for your goals? ASAHP. As soon as humanly possible.

If goals provide the drive and the fire in your belly, then standards allow the rubber to meet the road. Standards and goals are two sides of the coin, both essential for the overall outcome. A goal is a target. Action is required. But rather than jumping in like it's New Year and burning out a day or two later, we must determine the daily standards that must be in place for our goals to become reality. Standards are the daily boxes that must be ticked. They are lines in the sand, expectations of ourselves, and a commitment to settle for nothing less than what we've chosen to pursue.

MONEY DOESN'T GO FAR
WE MUST GO FURTHER

"If only I had 1 Million in the bank, I'd be set for life," you may have heard them say. However, 1 Million in the bank doesn't make you rich. It's not a small amount of money, granted, but if that's

the extent of your aspirations, you're in for a shock. 1 Million would allow you to pay down your debts, purchase a nice sensible home, treat yourself to a few toys, and live a number of years in moderate comfort before it ran out. You'd have to be careful with the money. You'd have to cover your taxes. You'd have the increased living costs of your new house and upgraded lifestyle. Whatever you did manage to hang onto, would slowly be eaten by inflation, and you certainly wouldn't be living off the interest.

I remember when my goal was to make £10,000 per month. When I finally achieved the magic number, I found myself with the same amount in the bank at the end of each month as I had when I was making significantly less, which is, not a lot. As your income rises, so do your expenses. I went from being the person who panicked about where we were going for dinner, to the person who offered to pay for everyone. I went from living in a tiny little house, to a stunning townhouse. I went from the Vauxhall Astra, to the new BMW. My cost of living went up. My taxes went up. The need to retain my new level of income in order to sustain the life I'd created for myself, was an ever-present concern.

Money really doesn't go far. Ask anyone who's made it. Unless you've been a few rounds and made the mistakes that most people are likely to make, you're going to realise that it's more important to put your money to work for you, and to build the base - than it is to drive expensive cars and live in luxurious houses.

However - and this is important - I don't imagine for one second that your goal is to live sensibly and retire rich. I remember reading a study in which it was highlighted that the majority of

American Millionaires drove Volvos. The general consensus of the study, a few years old now, was upon the importance of frugal living.

I don't know about you, but at no point have I woke up excited to go out and buy my dream Volvo or live within my means.

I wanted it all. I wanted the house, the cars, the toys, the travel, the holiday homes, the freedom, the security, the peace of mind, the expensive clothes, the exciting experiences, the ability to support those I cared about, the ability to contribute, and everything else that comes with it. I wanted it all. I wanted it fast. And if these things were collectively known as mistakes in the pursuit of greater wealth, then I wanted to make every mistake in the book. You only live once, and from the moment I woke up to wealth, I've wanted to make the most of every moment, and experience all that life had to offer. But how does that fit with being sensible?

There only is one solution. We must make more money. Money doesn't go far, so we must go further. If you wish to take a more measured and balanced approach, then I commend you for being here. If you're a little full-on like me and want it all, yesterday, then you too, are going to find exactly what you're looking for in this book.

Regardless of the outcome, we must all make it our mission to make more. Period. We must then balance our incoming funds in such a way that allows us to enjoy it based on the level we're playing at, whilst simultaneously putting the lions share back to work. Most working class people will have at least 1 Million pass through their hands over the course of their lives. Your new goal is to dramatically increase the pace at which this happens. It won't happen overnight, but it can happen much faster than you think.

I'm aware that many people do not equate money to happiness. I get it. Money in itself does not make you happy. What it does do, however, is allow you to buy freedom, peace of mind, security, and protection against life's unexpected challenges, recessions, Pandemics, and the unknown. It allows you to do some good in the world and enjoy more of what life has to offer. Those who don't think that money makes you happy, mostly consist of those who never had enough to know whether it did or didn't. I've been broke and I've been wealthy. I choose wealth every time.

Whatever you want, financial abundance must be at the forefront.

CHAPTER 2:
REPROGRAMMING FOR WEALTH

"I just can't imagine earning any less than $50,000 per month" he said. *"It just doesn't compute."* I glanced over, as he glared lazily into space. I remember it clearly. The Vegas strip lay low in the backdrop as we enjoyed lunch in the breathtaking hills of Anthem Country Club. The setting was perfect.

Hold that thought. Let's shift gears to a different conversation I had recently with a family member, who works in an administrative role. *"I can't apply for the £2,000 job when I've only been making £1,600 per month. It's too big a jump."*

Two highly contrasting positions, yet two illustrations of the inner game at play. We all have our unconscious limits on wealth; our ideas of where we belong in the world, and a level of comfort we can identify with.

Let's imagine either of these people lost their income. Do you think they'd kick back and settle for their new lot in life? Unlikely. Our $50,000 per month friend in Vegas is a $50,000 per month kind of guy, just as our £1,600 administrator is a £1,600 per month kind of girl. Both would find a way of recreating their version of normal.

When we witness the dramatic financial fall of any known Entrepreneur, only to see them rise again, you'll notice their comeback is not always in the same industry, or by similar means, and yet, despite the odds stacked against them, the majority of Entrepreneurs who fall, get back up again and reclaim their wealth. The strategy and approach are far less important than the Mindset of the individual.

We are where we are, and we are who we are. However, this is not a fixed reality. We can develop and grow, but it happens internally before it happens externally. When you raise your inner game, your outer game changes, and so too, do your results.

At Property Protege, we do a deep dive on your inner game of money. This is not a new idea. This has been discussed and taught by great minds alike for many years. The first time I came across the idea was in the New York Times best seller, "Secrets of The Millionaire Mind," (Piatkus 2007) by T Harv Eker. Harv goes into detail about our Financial Thermostat and Money Blueprint, as being at the core of our personal success. If you don't like the fruits, as Harv says, you must change the roots.

The idea then notably re-emerged in another of my favourite books, "I Can Make You Rich," (Hay House 2017) by Paul McKenna. Paul discusses how our unconscious mind has the number-one job of keeping us safe, by ensuring that today is as much like yesterday as possible. In this way, our unconscious works very much like a thermostat. If the room gets hotter than the set-point, the air conditioning would kick in and bring it back down to the comfort zone. Just as the only way to permanently change the temperature in the room is to reprogram the thermostat, the only way to permanently increase your wealth is to first reprogram your Wealth Thermostat.

WHERE ARE YOU?
AND HOW DID YOU GET THERE?

There are many elements that determine our inner game of wealth, and it hasn't happened overnight. From the moment you came into the world, you became a product of your environment, and subsequent environments thereafter. We all have our own minds, but we cannot help but be influenced by our families, friends, peers, surroundings, what we hear, see, and learn about the world and how to operate in it.

If you do not actively go to work on your inner game, then your past results are a great indicator of the future. Most people stay fairly static throughout their financial lives, not varying much in either direction. Getting by. Getting on. Then game over. Those who do create financial wealth, always do so through a continual process of inner growth and evolvement in how they process reality. There's the world, and then there's your world. Both are very different places.

So how did you arrive at your current reality?

Let's start by going way back. At the Property Protege Intensive, our 3-day live event which constitutes a substantial part of the 12-month programme, we ask each person in the room to write down the things they learned about money growing up, the beliefs they adopted, the patterns they saw, the lessons they learned. With the exception of one or two, the majority of people always identify as having come through similar experiences, which ultimately, for the most part, still direct many of their decisions.

Examples include beliefs such as, 'Money doesn't grow on trees,' 'Money is the root of all evil,' 'It takes money to make money,' 'The rich get richer,' 'If someone has money, then someone else had to loose it,' 'Rich people con people,' and my personal favourite, 'Making money is not for people like us.'

When I was growing up, we knew when my mum had extra money, because we had a takeaway that weekend, or we went to the cinema. As well intentioned as my mum was, the moment additional funds came in, they went straight back out the door again. Why? Because we deserved it. At least, that's what we believed.

I remember a few years back I had a little moment. I was on a winning streak. Deal after deal. Win after win. Life was going perfectly well. I remember thinking to myself, 'All good things must come to an end.' I caught myself midflow and stopped the thought dead in its tracks. All these years of progress and growth, and this nonsense still rears its head. I immediately countered it with a new belief, "I'm just getting warmed up." That felt much better. Back on track from there with the new reminder.

Our unconscious beliefs drive our thoughts and behaviour. We don't even know it's going on. But it's going on. Which is why we place such strong focus on first becoming aware of, and then changing those beliefs.

Let's ask another question to help establish our current position. Who are you spending your time with? After all, birds of a feather flock together. We tend to spend time with people like us. If your four best friends are fitness fanatics, you're likely the fifth. If your four best friends are gamers, you're likely the fifth. If your four best friends are Millionaires; well, you get the idea.

In April 2019, I flew to London to attend Tony Robbins' UPW. When I landed at City Airport, I received a phone call from someone I'd met a few months previous. Let's call him 'Steve.'
"Paul, are you in London?"
"I am now. Where are you?" I replied.
"Well, I've just been circling the city for 3 hours in a [private] jet. We've just signed a 100 Million deal for the Korean distribution rights to our product."

Of course, I was impressed, despite him telling me being 'less about' showing off, and more about a friend sharing a big win. I went along to a Docklands restaurant to meet Steve for drinks. It turned out I was crashing a management team dinner, but was made to feel very welcome. After a few rounds, I sat with Steve and we got to talking business. He asked me what my plans were, going forward.

Now at this point I have to take you back a few months. You see, the year before, my business partners and I flew to Miami to meet the man behind 10X, Grant Cardone. We featured on his show and streamed live to millions. We then signed a large cheque, and brought Grant to the UK in November 2018, filling the Intercontinental at the O2 with 2,000 people, and Glasgow's SEC, with another 500 people. We spoke at the event, as did Grant, and we all had a great time.

What many people don't realise, however, was that the upside wasn't in the profits. The upside was in the network we built throughout the campaign. For a start, having Grant Cardone in your phone book isn't a bad thing. We rubbed shoulders with celebrities who attended the events. We met many high-net worth individuals from a variety of industries. We attracted an abundance of opportunities and made many new friends, including Steve...

So when Steve asked me what I was planning to do next, he didn't expect anything less than what we'd done in the past. He expected more. I began to share some of my ideas. I talked of future events and some of the people I'd like to bring to the UK. I talked about changing the face of the seminar industry, moving the event space away from large scale pitch-fests focused on nothing but sales, to more value driven events with credible speakers. Steve listened intently. He smiled, nodded thoughtfully and knowingly, then opened his phone book, and showed me a list of serious A-listers, including presidents, movie stars, and several Billionaires. He told me he would back me, and invited me to his home a few weeks later, offering to assist.

How did someone like me, from a housing estate in Glasgow, end up rubbing shoulders with the likes of Steve, and gaining access to serious power players? Well, as I like to say, your network is your net worth, and frankly, it's impossible to walk away from conversations with people like Steve, feeling the same way about life.

When the conversation changes, so do the results. When you spend time around people who are more successful than you are, you cannot help but feel inspired, challenged, and driven for more. Sometimes, you can even feel like an imposter. When I was in my early twenties, starting out on the journey, I'd find every opportunity to get close and talk to successful people. Every time without fail, I left the conversation feeling like my goals were laughable, and that there was a much bigger game at play.

So I'll ask again. Who are *you* spending time with? What does the conversation look like? Do you leave feeling inspired, driven, challenged, focused, and ready to take your life to new heights? Or does it look somewhat different to what's being discussed here?

They say that you are the average of the four or five people you spend the most time with. So with that in mind, what's the average financial worth, or levels of income, of those people? I'm not suggesting you cut or change your friends, as such, but that you look for the opportunity to make more new friends, and become very conscious about what and who you're letting in. You won't necessarily start by finding a Steve, but you'll start where you're at and work your way up.

So what else affects our inner game?

If our deeply rooted beliefs are silently running the show, and our circle of friends are impacting our direction, then next we must look at how we're fuelling our minds.

What are you taking in? What are you mentally consuming day to day? Are you listening to educational podcasts and audiobooks, reading industry related news, studying biographies and financial reports? Or are you consuming the latest radio wind-up, the morning news, drowning in BS on social, following agenda-driven media, and catching the latest scandal from the local tabloid?

What are you putting into that mind of yours? Whatever you focus on, you attract, and whatever you focus on, you ultimately become.

Other questions you can ask yourself...

What has your bank account looked like over the past 3 months and beyond? Are there visible patterns? Are the next 3 months predictable by the looking at the last? How much money could you lose, right now, without freaking out over it? Could you be playing a more aggressive game? Are you hitting your capacity financially, feeling overwhelmed, or hitting your personal ceiling? How does your future look based on living life in accordance with what we learned about wealth and money growing up? How does your environment affect your ability to perform and grow?

FINANCIAL REPROGRAMMING

It's important that we ask ourselves difficult questions. When we're physically out of shape and we look in the mirror, there's no denying reality. Unfortunately most people avoid looking in the financial mirror, choosing instead to sedate and put their head in the sand. It's always a convenient idea that it's not our fault that we are where we are, that it's someone else's responsibility, that someone or something else is to blame. It's easier to justify or complain, than it is to accept responsibility for our lot in life. But only when we begin to look clearly at where we're at and how we got there, from a place of ownership, can we begin to make important changes in our Mindset and take new steps towards increasing our Wealth Thermostat and financial capacity.

A COMMITMENT TO GROWTH

I'm an avid learner. I love to listen to podcasts and audiobooks in particular. I find it easier to consume content this way. When people ask me what they should study or listen to, or read, I have two thoughts that I share with them.

The first thought, is that they study both content related to their industry, and content that reaches into the minds of the greats. I love to learn from the giants who walked before us, as well as the modern-day titans of wealth and success. I want to know what makes or made them tick. I understand all too well that it's not the strategies employed that come first. What comes first is the Mindset of the individuals to allow all else to happen.

The second thought that I share, is to stop jumping from idea to idea, and instead, focus on repeatedly consuming and deep learning of that which stood out to them. Don't read 1,000 books once. Read a couple of books a thousand times. Master what you're learning. For example, if the content in this book resonates with you, make it your companion. Rip it apart, sentence by sentence. Read beyond the lines and find deeper meaning. You can't read the same book twice and have the same experience. Each time you return, you consume it from a new perspective.

Consuming relevant content while continually learning is a phenomenal way to begin to reprogram your Wealth Thermostat. The entrepreneurs of a few decades past, had to figure it out themselves. Today, on the other hand, we have countless books and resources available to us, where those who've gone before us, have literally mapped out their journey in pain staking detail, giving us every advantage to succeed. When you continually consume such content, you cannot help but have your mind begin to change automatically, raising your inner game, and overcoming what holds you back.

In order for our income to grow, *we* must grow. A commitment to personal growth through knowledge is vital. What matters more, however, is the correct application of that knowledge. Many people mistake personal development for consumption alone. True personal development is achieved in applying what we learn.

SURROUND YOURSELF WITH WINNERS

Day to day life for me, as I grew up, didn't lend the opportunity to find myself around highly successful people. As someone who has always questioned life and wanted more from it, I'd naturally attach myself to the handful of people I came across over the years who were in my eyes at the time, more successful than I was.

You find an uncle who can fix cars. It's exciting to watch. You look up to them, put them on a pedestal, and find yourself amazed at their ability. An awesome uncle, who you love spending time with. A role model. You get the idea. A cool uncle, however, in context of discussing financial life progression, is only useful in terms of the lessons imparted based on what they do, how they do it, and the general attitude that comes with it. If you want to become a car mechanic, then the cool uncle who fixes cars is perfect.

But what if your goal was to make the elusive Million we discussed earlier? Well, wouldn't it make sense to find yourself around those who've done it, or those who are aggressively pursuing it, and speak the same language? You can find the words of the wise in countless books and audiobooks etc, but nothing beats discovering you are capable of being influenced by those who've walked the walk in person. Remember, when the conversation changes, so do the results. You can only see what you can see, based on where you've been and your own life experience, but there's always another level. And when you achieve that next level, there's another level still.

When you start with nothing, a £10,000 windfall seems like a staggering amount of money. £100,000 seems like a dream. £1,000,000 can seem unimaginable. But what about when you do achieve your first Million? For a start, you instantly become the most successful among your friends and family. However, stand beside someone with Ten Million, and you've barely even started. It's important not to get caught in the trap of comparing ourselves with others, but what I'm illustrating here is the matter of perspective in terms of your own idea of subjective success.

What we're also discussing here, is a very important lesson that aids the rich. If you've made a Million, then just as we were discussing earlier, it becomes much less of a mental leap to do it again. Equally, with your 7 figures in the bank, the idea of chasing after deals that net you a mere £10,000 seems small time. Your thinking expands. Your capacity increases. Make sense? I hope so, because this is a large part why it's important to find ourselves around those more financially successful than we are. Not so we can put them on a pedestal and worship them, but so we can let their Mindset rub off on us, so we can run our ideas past them, so we can begin to adopt the standard traits of those who've achieved what we would like to achieve.

By surrounding ourselves with those who've achieved, we get to grow by default, as we find ourselves influenced by people we respect who've made it happen. High performers, achievers, winners, share the same mental makeup. They speak the same language. Read any book in any field of endeavour written by winners, and you'll find the same attitudes and general Mindset principles again and again.

How can you get yourself around more successful people? Such people don't even have to be millionaires, but must certainly have been successful by your own measures. Be careful to avoid those who appear successful but are more show than tell. When I first started thinking like this, I began to realise there were a number of people already within my expanded network through friends of friends that I could begin to tap into. I joined high end health clubs. I became conscious over where I spent my time and who with. I became aware that I was always on stage, telling the world how to treat me and who I was, and began to attract better company. I attended networking events. I joined business breakfasts. I attended workshops and seminars and always pulled together the funds for the front row seats in order to be around others of a similar Mindset. Every opportunity, I took full advantage. You can do the same.

Another route to explore is to tap into our community at Property Protege, known to its members as the Tribe. Our Tribe are a focused group of individuals who help one another, joint venture with one another, and share advice based on their wins and their lessons learned within our private group and the weekly zoom calls that form part of the Property Protege Programme. Nothing beats having direct access to a like-minded group of individuals on the same mission that you are, with some at the same level, and others further down the line. Whether you join our Tribe or find another, it's vital to tap into a peer group that will support your direction and help you get there faster.

IMMERSE YOURSELF IN SUCCESS

Let's discuss the pros and cons of social media in terms of what we're discussing here. If you're like most people, your Facebook feed is overrun by people sharing information that has absolutely no relevance to your life, and serves as nothing more than a convenient distraction. Of course there's bound to be some good content on there, but generally speaking, your school friends, people you barely know, and distant family you've spoken to once, shouldn't have a casting vote in your stance on life. It's impossible not to find ourselves caught up in the opinions and worldview of others if that's what we're seeing each day. Similarly LinkedIn, an apparent professional platform that features little more than lots of people making noise. Instagram, SnapChat, TikTok, YouTube. Fantastic tools of distraction, which isn't a bad thing, if you're looking to be entertained and distracted. But in terms of business, we must use such platforms first to inspire and light up our lives, and second, from a producer point of view as opposed to the consumer; as tools for growth.

I'm going to recommend that you unfollow everyone and everything, then go back and refollow only those people and pages that matter to you. Then, go and actively follow those people and pages that make you feel alive. Whatever success is to you, immerse yourself in it. If you like expensive watches, cars, and luxury living, go and follow profiles on Instagram and Facebook that focus on nothing but expensive watches, cars, and luxury living. If you like to see updates on close family whilst at the office, make sure you follow close family. If you enjoy reading trending information on Property, start following relevant hashtags on

LinkedIn. The important note to remember here, is to follow people and pages that light you up, inspire you, and make you feel alive. Let your social feeds become a welcome distraction that accelerate your life and contribute to your success, and then ensure you don't allow those distractions to become the detriment to your progress.

HAVE A LITTLE FUN WITH IT

Fun activities could be to test drive the dream car, or view your dream home. I remember test driving a Bentley before I ever owned one. I arrived at the Bentley garage in my Vauxhall Astra, and of course, parked it around the corner so the salesman wouldn't see it. I wore a suit so they would take me more seriously. Ridiculous, I know. When I sat in the car, before the salesman joined me, I had what Dan Pena calls a 'smell the leather experience.' I felt the stitching on the wheel, I adjusted the car to fit me, I smelled the fresh new-car leather. I started it up and felt her purr to life, the vibration of an engine beyond that of my Astra, beating the heart of my dream. I felt alive. I took the Bentley out on the road, put my foot down when we reached the motorway, and was gently pulled against my seat as we flew down the M74. When I arrived back at the Bentley garage, I'd tasted what I wanted, and I wanted more of it.

Similarly, I remember visiting show homes, telling the agent I'd be inside having a look, only for them to find me an hour later lying on the bed pretending it was mine. I would go home, study floor plans, and visualise living my dream life in my dream home.

I'd become so lost in my visualisations that I didn't want to come back out.

It's important to appreciate what you have, and take nothing for granted, whilst simultaneously driving towards more of what you want. One life. Live it.

KNOW YOUR VALUE

It's important to understand that test driving the dream car and viewing the dream home aren't necessarily about the car or the home. It's about knowing your worth and knowing your value. It's about understanding that you have every opportunity to go after whatever you want in life, in the knowledge that if others have done it, and many of them, then it's very possible for you too. The past does not equal the future, and we literally have a blank canvas upon which to paint.

Someone may ask, *"Who are you to achieve success?"* I prefer, *"Who are you NOT to?"* Never live your life based on the limitations of other people. Never live your life based on your own limiting beliefs of what's possible. Instead, find examples of what you would love to have your life be about, understand that it *can* happen, get your Mindset in check, follow the principles in this book, and get after it.

Our deepest fear is not that we are inadequate.
Our deepest fear is that we are powerful beyond measure.
It is our light, not our darkness that most frightens us.

We ask ourselves, who am I to be brilliant, gorgeous, talented, fabulous?

Actually, who are you not to be?

You are a child of God.

Your playing small does not serve the world.

There is nothing enlightened about shrinking so that other people won't feel insecure around you.

We are all meant to shine, as children do.

We were born to make manifest the glory of God that is within us.

It's not just in some of us; it's in everyone.

And as we let our own light shine, we unconsciously give other people permission to do the same.

As we are liberated from our own fear, our presence automatically liberates other.

- Marianne Williamson

ACKNOWLEDGE, REPROGRAM, ACCELERATE

Once you know where you're at, and how you got there, you officially reach ground zero. From this place of acknowledgement, understanding, and awareness, we can begin to immerse ourselves in more of what we want. We surround ourselves with those further down the path, we soak in the lessons of those who've gone before us through audiobooks and podcasts, we learn from a Tribe of peers focused on similar outcomes, we find mentors and support, we follow people and pages that inspire us and drive us forward, we attend events and meetings and conferences where we can continually learn and grow. We literally become sponges for new ways of thinking and being, that make us more of the best part of who we are, and who we are supposed to be.

Reprogramming is in fact a process of conditioning. The learning never stops. The growth never stops. And although you will continue to evolve, it's all too easy to let old patterns and thinking slip in. Never stop learning. Never stop growing. Never stop.

Life is exciting. A whole world of opportunity awaits. Let's continue.

CHAPTER 3:
WHAT STOPS YOU?

Ask most people what they want, and you'll hear what they'd like, and believe they could possibly have, as opposed to what they would *truly* want if they knew they could not fail. Hopefully by this point in the book you'll be clearer on what you *actually* want, and understand that it's in our own minds where we must release the brakes. We also now know the importance of reprogramming and reconditioning, and why we must continue to learn, evolve, and grow, in line with what we want.

So if you *know* what you want, why don't you have it?

What stops you?

Because if nothing was stopping you, you'd already have it.

Which then forms the second part of the equation. *"I want X, but..."* We then insert the reason or reasons as to why we believe we cannot have what we want.

Sometimes it's due to the opinions of other people. Sometimes we lack the belief. Sometimes it's about finding the time.

Sometimes it's about life balance. Sometimes it's about finding the deals. Sometimes it's about finding the money. Sometimes it's about finding the motivation. Sometimes it's about finding the courage. Sometimes it's about getting the right information. Sometimes it's about finding the right support. Sometimes it's about Global Pandemics, Recessions, and Coronaviruses.

What you're going to realise as we move through this book, is that there are ways and means to move forward despite all of the above. Remember, it's not what happens that makes the difference, but what you choose to do with what happens, and the meaning you choose to attach to it. Also, it's never a question of resources, but a matter of resourcefulness. My core question to you now, is, *'What would you do if you knew you could not fail?'* Of course, you can fail, but even failure should be taken as part of the journey, and reinterpreted as 'lessons along the way.' As the late great Jim Rohn would say, *"Never wish life was easier; wish that you were better."*

No matter what happens or how successful you become, you're always going to face challenges in Property, and the bigger you get, the bigger the challenges will become. Problems aren't going anywhere. They're here to stay. This book is a catalyst for both those just getting starting, and those who are significantly further down the line, in overcoming the primary obstacles and challenges that most people face; but even out-with what you'll find in this book, you're going to face some proper nightmares. Sounds fun, right? That's life. Step up and move on.

I once heard it said that if you're facing big problems, you're being a small person. With only a handful of extreme exceptions to this rule, I would agree entirely. It's a matter of perspective. For example, £10,000 is a lot of money to someone with nothing, whereas £10,000 is less impactful to someone with ten to one hundred times that number. In the same way, an apparent big challenge in Property to someone who's never experienced it before, is a small matter of daily routine to someone who's been playing the game much longer, and has grown in their capacity and experience.

What most people don't realise, is that they are nothing more than a handful of comfort zone stretches away from what they want. If you've never gone through challenges before, step up and push through it. Soon, it'll become part of your everyday reality. I'm going to help you in this book. We're going to address the big ones. By the end of it, you'll find yourself with every reason for success, and very few reasons, if any, for why you cannot have what you want.

100% RESPONSIBILITY

On the topic of what stops us, I have a confession to make. I was once a massive victim. Life happened to me, I didn't create my life. I did what victims do. I blamed. I complained. I justified. There's an obvious challenge with this. It didn't get me anywhere. Nothing changed as a result. Whenever we allow ourselves to blame, complain or justify, we may feel better, or detached from the event itself, but it doesn't move us forward. It's nothing more than noise, negative energy, and wasted thought.

Successful people do not assume the victim role. Successful people take responsibility. They choose to take life's challenges and redefine them as 'lessons along the way.' There's no blaming. There's no complaining. There's no justification. There's 100% responsibility for their life and their results.

If you aren't in control, then who is? If you aren't responsible for what happens to you, then who is? If you're not driving the bus, then who is?

Victim mentality is an absolute killer of dreams. I've watched it destroy ambition, hope, desire, and results. I've watched it stop people dead in their tracks. I've watched it allow good people to fall back into old patterns and belief systems, and shun their previous aspirations in Property and business.

The problem we have, is that playing the victim is the easy way out. It's much more difficult to put your hand up and say, "It's on me," but when we take ownership, and assume responsibility for whatever happens to us, good or bad, we find ourselves in the unique position of being able to direct our lives. Most people give themselves a pat on the back when things go right, but rarely accept responsibility for the alternative.

A few years back, I was involved in a number of deals with a small group of joint venture partners. Standard situation. Something I've done many times. Unfortunately, one of the joint venture partners in this particular setup began to give off little red flags. The warning signs continued. I carried on regardless. We later found out that this person has caused some serious trouble and left the rest of us holding the responsibility. This person went back to their life, with hundreds of thousands of pounds that they did not earn or deserve, leaving myself and my partners with the drama of fixing an additional hundreds of thousands of pounds worth of issues. Fun times.

I remember a friend asking if I felt regret over joint venturing with this person. It was in that moment that I realised how far I'd come. Not for one second did I feel regret, or disappointment, or even a level of anger, which would be perfectly justifiable. I could have complained. I could have blamed. I would have been well within my rights to blow off some steam. But I didn't. The reality is, I chose to go into the joint venture with this individual. I should have been more thorough in my due diligence. I ignored the red flags and warning signs. It was my mistake. I am at a fault for what happened. Now that doesn't make sense to most, but it does to me. If I'm not responsible, then I've let life take me for a ride and I shouldn't be in business. Instead, I learned some painful lessons, I fixed what was within my control, and continued to move forward.

Two beliefs that help me through life, are as follows.

'I create my life. Life doesn't happen to me.'

And, 'Life happens for me, not to me.'

Notice in both beliefs, that at no point does life happen to me. It happens as a result of my decisions, choices and actions. I also believe that whatever life sends my way, that *'the obstacle is the way.'* Whatever happens, I must find the advantage and opportunity that it presents. We can always find the negative in any situation, but in my mind, there's always a positive too, and that's where I choose to focus.

I remember one of my mentors sharing a status on Facebook. It went along the lines of, "Celebrate your success, because you are exactly where you've chosen to be. The relationship you're in, your health, your fitness, your income, your life. Every choice and decision you've made has led you to where you are right now. Celebrate. You are exactly where you are supposed to be."

A sore one to take perhaps, but a lesson in personal responsibility. Own your results. They're yours. Life is a result. You create your life. Life happens for you, and very rarely to you. Whatever comes your way, claim it, learn from it, and use it.

WE GET WHAT WE WORK FOR

At Property Protege, there's a moment where we show a blank piece of paper on the screen. A little tongue in cheek perhaps, and a running joke, but we highlight that on this blank piece of paper, is everything that you are entitled to, deserve, should expect, and have coming. The reality is, there's not a lot we deserve other than what we work for. There's very little we should expect, other than what we work for. There's very little we have coming to us, other than what we work for. Do you see the pattern here? When we get past the idea that life, or society, or the government, or an employer, or anyone for that matter is responsible for looking after us, and we realise that we get what we work for; at that point, we actually have a chance of making it.

Beyond the public sector, we are entitled to very little. And yet, in our modern society, far too many people expect something for little or nothing.

That's not how business works. It's not how Property works. If you want something, you must move past this lower level thinking, take complete responsibility, and understand that it's entirely on you to go out and get it.

A COMMITMENT TO SUCCESS

Commitment is like pregnancy. You're pregnant. Or you're not pregnant. At no point in my wife's pregnancies did she tell me that she was tired that day and was taking the night off. Nope. She was all-in for the duration. That's how it works.

Commitment is no different. We're either all in or not at all. There are no half-measures. There is no 'we'll see,' or 'I'll try.' This is Property. Through Property Protege and other resources, you have the strategies and the roadmap. Through this book and other resources, you can develop the Mindset. Countless others have made it happen. It's possible. So why not you? If you want it then lets commit here and now. No more half measures. No more dabbling. No more watching from the sidelines while others make it.

Don't think and grow rich. Just do it.

Let's address the obstacles that hold us back. One by one.

By the end of this book, you'll have no excuses, no reasons why not, no justifications, and no obstacles in your way. What you will have, is a clear path, an abundance of opportunity, and a blank canvas upon which to paint. It's going to be an eye opener. It's going to be a breath of fresh air. Everything you've wanted, starts now.

CHAPTER 4:
PANDEMICS, RECESSIONS AND ACTS OF GOD

At the time of writing, we're on week two of lockdown in the UK due to Covid-19. At times like this, leaders from all backgrounds and all walks of life have been forced to step up. As such, I've been more active in our Property Protege Facebook community than ever before. Whilst society pushes through a phenomenal amount of uncertainty, many people have many questions, and it's my job to help my clients navigate where possible. So whilst there are various elements of what's being discussed by Property and Business pundits that will fluctuate and change, I want to give you a very stoic and level view of the playing field, with advice and information that will remain unchanging, whether you're reading this in April 2020, or January 2030. This was never intended as part of the book, but as it's a dominating force at present, it would be an injustice not to share what I see, and why I'm upbeat about the opportunities a situation such as this presents.

When things go wrong, on a National or Global scale, including Pandemics, Recession, and Acts of God (otherwise defined as events that occur outside of human control that cannot be predicted,) we can look at them in various ways.

What most people do, is allow the situation to consume them. They don't see the situation as it is, they see it as *they* are, or, much worse than it is. Bad news sells, and in tough times there's no shortage of media looking for the most scandalous or fear-based headlines. We face fear and uncertainty. There are mixed views and opinions. One government, authority, or voice of expertise suggests one approach, whilst another government, authority, or voice of expertise suggests another. Our families, friends, and social media, provide an endless onslaught of thought and theory. All people can talk about is what's going on, and it seems like there's no light at the end of the tunnel. So what do we do? We go into defence mode. We look after ourselves. We shutdown, and hope that someone smarter than us will fix the situation. Whatever that situation may be.

That's one approach. The most common for sure.

Another approach we can choose to take when life deals an unexpected or all-consuming blow, is to step up and lead. To be a voice of inspiration. To be a source of strength. To focus on the positive whilst acknowledging its opposite. To play our part. To be responsible. To ask ourselves what we can do to support others. To keep a level head and focus on what is within our control, as opposed to what is not.

Everything passes in time. We are a resilient species. We've weathered the Antonine Plague, the Black Death, the Pneumonic Plague, the Spanish Flu, La Pesadilla, the Hong Kong Flu, Swine Flu, and much more, not to mention World Wars, The Great Depression, recessions, natural disasters, and the vast catalogue of historic scenarios that knocked societies, industries, and economies on their head. Ecclesiastes said, *"What has been, will be again. What has been done, will be done again. There is nothing new under the sun,"* The more things change, the more they stay the same. This isn't the first time we've faced a Global Pandemic or challenge of this scale. It certainly won't be the last. We've come through worse, and will go through worse, yet still. *This too, shall pass.*

What we currently face is a call to action, to step up; to realise that it's not what happens that defines us, it's how we choose to respond to what happens, the meaning we choose to give to what happens, and what we choose to do about it. We must choose to see situations for what they are; nothing more, nothing less, and continue to do what we can throughout.

What we face is serious. There's no denying that, and we must all do our part. At the same time, whilst many choose to be consumed, we instead, can choose to adapt and refocus. At the time of writing, as we work to flatten the curve of Covid-19, we have an opportunity to reinvent ourselves, to study, to learn new skills, to exercise, to get our health in check, to balance the books, to cut our expenses, to gain perspective, to find where we've been weak and tighten our belts, to innovate and recreate, to trim the fat, to spend time with our families, to learn to take nothing for granted, and to stand on our own two feet.

RECESSIONS AND PROPERTY

For several years, I've been sharing my views and predictions on an upcoming recession. This is something I have a deep personal interest in, and over the last year or so in particular, all of the signs, indicators, trends, and the voices of experience from leading economists, financial analysts and so forth, have been pointing towards the same thing. Many have been referring to what's coming as an ultimate all-time reset, a Great Depression. A recession is an economic term for a business cycle contraction where there is a decline in economic activity, brought about by a variety of causes. Go back far enough, and you'll see a consistent and almost predictable cycle on repeat over the decades.

With the emergence of Covid-19, we've seen a devastating impact on our Global economy. We've seen a devastating impact on SME's (Small and Medium Enterprise), which represent 50% of GDP and 98% of private sector employment. We've seen a significant drop in widespread spending. We've seen Bailouts and Government Stimulus normally reserved for kick-starting growth and financially re-stimulating the economy during a recession. We've seen central banks worldwide adding new money into the economy through Quantitative Easing. With such drastic last measures in motion, there are no more cards left to play. Not to mention that we've now seen interest rates being cut to all-time lows, with the UK at the time of writing now slashed to 0.1%, with some European Countries in negative interest rates.

If we were on track for a recession before, imagine what it's going to look like in times to come, in the wake and aftermath of

Covid-19. Normally, a Global recession will work its way from country to country and market to market, with the impact being felt more in different places at different times. As it stands now, however, we're all in it together.

So how does this affect Property?

Property fluctuates at a much slower pace than stocks, shares, and other markets. It is by-and-large governed by supply and demand. Where we'll see the biggest impact on Property prices, will be as a result of the effects a recession (and Covid-19) on employment and income.

During the 1930's, at the height of the Great Depression, 1 in 4 people were out of work. In a recent two-week period, unemployment in the US reached 1 in 16 people; and at the time of writing, we aren't even in the thick of it yet. As for those who are in a position to keep their jobs, over 75% have had their income cut by at least 20%, in a world where 78% of people are living month to month, with little or no savings, investments, or safeguards against the unknown, and require 100% of their income to stay afloat, pay their debts, and put food on the table. The tide has gone out, and most people are swimming naked.

Jobs will come back in time. The economy will recover in time. People will find their way back to employment. These things are for sure. It will take time, but the damage will come to pass. How long that will take, has yet to be seen. What's also unclear, is how long it will take to see spending return to normal. We can't tell how long it will take to see people go back to concerts, movies, sporting events, music festivals, and travel, in the way that they did before, in terms of both affordability, and changes in the way we spend; not to mention the recovery process in the wake of Covid-19 and any form of accompanying recession.

It will play out, however it plays out.

But at this point, what I want to focus on, in line with the theme of this book, is the opportunity that our current predicament presents to those of us in Property.

TOUGH TIMES PRESENT MASSIVE OPPORTUNITY

There's no denying the hugely damaging effects we are witnessing on our Global economy, on business, on society, on individuals, on life itself. There's no denying it. But there's also no fighting it, in terms of wishing it were different. It's not different. It's here. It's happening. We must accept it, and choose to find deeper meaning, to find the good, and to find the opportunities that 'whatever life throws at us' presents.

Remember, life happens *for* you, not *to* you. *You* create your life.

What's detrimental in Property for the average person, presents an opportunity for the Investor. In essence, you have a crystal ball, because you know the effects our current situation is having on the world around us. You also know we're facing recession in the very near future. As a result, countless people are going to find themselves in financial difficulty, at varying degrees, and facing other challenges, as a result of the pressure brought on by the financial difficulty. People in such situations will find themselves in a position where they will want to (or in most cases *have* to) sell their Property fast. What was once the family home, is now a burden, or an asset which can be offloaded to mend other fences. People in such situations are known as motivated sellers, and generally don't have the luxury of time to sell on the open market, requiring a quick solution through a private sale.

Armed with a variety of strategies, options and exits, this is where the Investor comes in. The Investor can make quick decisions. They are able to acquire the Property at a much quicker pace. The Investor has the tools and resources at their disposal to solve complicated problems that sellers may find themselves facing. The Investor can help the seller, and fast. The upside to the Investor, is the opportunity to purchase a Property where value can be added, where a discount can be attained; and when prices begin to fall, to purchase a Property at a significantly reduced market value. In recent years, when the market has been up, this is how Investors have operated regardless. In down times, however, which we currently face, and which we will dive further into, this process will accelerate exponentially, presenting even more opportunity for Investors.

ETHICAL INVESTING

During the last downturn, I personally did hundreds of deals. Some deals were added to my personal portfolio; many deals which did not fit my criteria were packaged up and traded *(in other words sold)* to other Investors. I achieved all of this, by finding out how I could help the seller, as opposed to taking advantage of their situation. Many people are unethical in their approach. They know the seller is motivated and is facing difficult circumstances, and they push to find out how much of a discount they can squeeze. I have always taken the opposite approach, and teach and expect the same of those in our Property Protege Programme. The ethical way of doing business in Property, is to truly listen to the seller, to find out more about their situation, to discover their challenges, and to seek to find a variety of options in order to truly help them.

Whether you are the Investor, or you are sourcing deals and selling them to Investors, what you're going to find is that when you truly set out to help people, they will pass you referral after referral. I can assure you of this because it has happened to me more times than I can count, and I see it regularly with our Property Proteges. In the difficult times we face, more and more people are going to need your help. Help them with compassion and care, and you'll find yourself with more opportunity than you can handle.

NOW IS THE TIME TO ACCELERATE IN PROPERTY

I started in Property just before the last recession took effect. For me, I had no idea what was about to happen, but was acutely aware that some of my more intelligent and successful peers in Property were positioning themselves for what was to come. I paid close attention and followed suit. Armed with the right knowledge, I was able to kickstart my success in Property, produce serious cash flow, and begin to build substantial wealth, all in difficult times, through helping other people in tough situations.

The reality is, *any* time is a good time to get started. Property is your number 1 vehicle for financial success. However, whilst any time is a good time to get started, there are times when opportunity comes more abundantly. When times get tough, recessions loom, Global Pandemics turn our worlds upside down, and Acts of God test humanity, those times, are the most opportune moments to help other people, and in turn, build our own wealth.

CHAPTER 5:
THE GOOD OPINION OF OTHER PEOPLE

The phone rang. I was nervous. I was excited. I was 21 years old and had just recorded my first video about Property. It wasn't easy. It took hours of filming and countless failed attempts. My sister held our old Flip Cam, her hands numb from the amount of time it took. We filmed in my mum's hall, doing our best to avoid the ripped wallpaper. It got as good as it was going to get. I logged into Facebook and shared the video I'd uploaded to YouTube, which offered to help those who were struggling to sell their Property.

I picked up the phone. *"Hi, Paul McFadden here..."* I began, before being pushed down by a louder voice, *"Is this Paul McFadden? Paul, you're a dickhead."* Group laughter followed, then the line went dead. One of my so-called friends was prank calling after seeing my video. Despite being the first time, it wouldn't be the last.

It's not a nice feeling. Neither is knowing that your friends are talking about you. Neither is being judged based on your age. Neither is being laughed at by estate agents. Neither is being lectured about being a dreamer by well-meaning in-laws. Neither is being told at every turn to get a real job, get a grip, get a life. Neither is walking into a family party to jeers of *"There's Paul the Millionaire, are you rich yet Paul?"*

There's a long list buried in a dark corner of my mind, of the abuse, the criticism, the insults, the attacks, the sarcasm, and everything else I've had to contend with, more so from the early years. It doesn't bother me now, which is good, because unfortunately, it also doesn't stop. Over a decade later, and I endure more abuse and hate now than I ever did back then. It's no longer friends and family; it's speculators and pundits, it's people on social media who don't even know me, it's people who have a superficial understanding of Property, it's people who judge me by my car or home, and people who think Investors are vultures.

It never stops. It never will.

Sometimes you'll feel downtrodden. Sometimes your blood will boil. Sometimes it will create doubt. Sometimes it will create fear. Sometimes it will make you feel you've been foolish. Sometimes you'll feel like going back to your place in the world. Sometimes you'll feel like everyone is against you. And whether the source is friends, family, your partner, social media, or the world around you, I get it, it sucks.

WHY DOES IT HAPPEN?

We live in a diverse world; a shared space, with 7.8 Billion souls, all with their own unique beliefs, references, ideas, life experiences, blueprints, and stories to tell. It's what makes the world such an interesting place, but also a primary underlying driver of conflict.

We can look at other people and consider them negative, haters, or critics. Or, we can realise that they're not necessarily being negative, hating, or criticising; they're simply coming from a different viewpoint, place, or perspective.

The next time you're on social media, look at what fuels conversation. What you'll see, are people agreeing with each other, sharing their take on what was said, or disagreeing with each other. Whether written, or expressed through an opinion-based 'like' button, everything comes down to subjectivity; in the form of personal perception. If there was no room for agreement, disagreement, or shared experience, there would be no need to communicate.

Of course, there are some people who seem to genuinely hate, who are unnecessarily negative or critical, who seem to get-off on the failure of others. Again, it would be easy to label, but unless you've done something to personally offend them, or they have in someway misinterpreted what you do, or they're simply tarring you with the same brush as others; it's important to realise that what you're seeing is generally not a reflection of you, but a reflection of what's going on in their world. Some people had it rough growing up. Some people have day-to-day challenges. Some people have had negative experiences with others who do what you do. Some people just need to vent. In truth, I feel for them.

Unfortunately, misery loves company. Just as *you* are upgrading your own peer group and attracting the right sort of people into your world; negative people, particularly online, also seem to find one another, which only amplifies the noise.

When you get started in Property, or you choose to accelerate, other people are going to know about it; your nearest and dearest, your social circle, those you have professional dealings with, those who see your content or new direction online, and so on. You don't even have to open your mouth to incite the 'good' opinion of other people, but when you do; expect an onslaught of unsolicited feedback. Don't expect to like or dislike what's said. The opinions of others are none of your business. They are what they are. It is what it is.

People don't see you as you are, they see you as *they* are. Remember that. Remove the emotion, and do as Churchill said; Keep Calm, and Carry On.

ENSURE YOUR NEAREST AND DEAREST ARE ONSIDE

Of course, in most cases, it's the people closest to us who have their word first. Sometimes it's through care or concern. Other times it's through fear, insecurity, or a lack of understanding. Perhaps they are basing your possibilities on their limitations. Perhaps they have their own idea of how Property should be done. Perhaps they've tried their hand at business in the past and failed. There are many scenarios and possibilities.

I remember the days when I was finding my feet in Property. After realising just how vital it was to work 'on me,' to develop my Mindset, and to learn and to grow; I began attending personal development seminars with speakers and trainers such as Tony Robbins, T Harv Eker, and Christopher Howard. As you might expect, this didn't always go down well with the people around me, including my partner at the time.

These people, whom I cared for, and who cared deeply for me, didn't understand why I was travelling the world, attending seminars, and scraping money together to fund my 'education.' They didn't understand why I was willing to leave a perfectly good job to step into the unknown. They didn't understand why I couldn't just settle down, appreciate what I had, and get on with life. I knew that some of them felt fear *for* me, whilst others felt fear of who I was becoming, and perhaps, of being left behind. It's important to remember that when you stretch your comfort zone, you simultaneously stretch and unsettle the people around you, and their ideas of normality and comfort.

If you care for your nearest and dearest, then you must appreciate that they might not understand your new direction, ambitions, aspirations, and desires. Your new ways of thinking may frighten them, intimidate them, or worry them. You must keep this in mind. My number 1 recommendation for those with close friends and family who are less than supportive or lacking perspective, is that you adequately communicate with them.

It's not always vital that your partner or loved ones understand what you're doing, but it's absolutely essential that they give you the space to do it. To ensure you have this space, and their backing and confidence, you must take the time to share the big picture. Find the right moment, or create the right moment, and enrol them in your vision. Paint the picture for them. Share your reasons. Help them understand the deeper meaning behind the pursuit. By doing so, they'll gain a deeper understanding, you'll have a chance to allay their fears and concerns, and you'll find it a much smoother ride going forward.

LET GO OF THE NEED TO BE LIKED

It's important to help your nearest and dearest understand what you're doing. What matters much less, however, are the thoughts and opinions of your wider circle, as well as those you barely know, or don't know at all, in the wider online and offline worlds around you. You're going to realise that everyone has an opinion, and most often, those with the strongest opinions, are those with the least experience to share them.

The fact of the matter is, however, what other people think of you, is none of your business. I once heard it said that 'high performance people don't care what you think of them.' Richard Branson doesn't go home upset that Joe Bloggs had a little rant about him on Facebook. Bill Gates doesn't call it a day because a hate group was formed in his name. Warren Buffet doesn't lose sleep because you don't respect his take on investment. Of course, customer and market feedback can and generally will be heard, but even still, high performers generally take a strong personal stance on what they believe in, and will push forward despite public opinion for the greater good, as they see it.

The opposite approach is to be a people-pleaser. Abraham Lincoln once said, "You can please some of the people all of the time, you can please all of the people some of the time, but you can't please all of the people all of the time."

No matter what you do in life, you're going to upset people.

It is what it is.

I used to be a people-pleaser. I couldn't handle if someone was upset with me. I had to fix the situation. I couldn't sleep knowing others were coming against me. I couldn't focus when I knew people were talking about me. I wanted everyone to like me. I was upset when people tried to hurt me in business. I let the world outside of me, affect the world inside me. Unfortunately, to wish things like this were any different is to live in fantasy land.

What other people think of you is none of your business. For every person laughing at you publicly, there are ten more laughing at you privately. We must accept it, and move on.

Two things that helped me get over my need to allow the opinions of others to dominate my life are as follows. First, when I found out that President Obama won by 50.5% of the vote. Imagine going into work tomorrow and 49.5% of your colleagues didn't want you to be there. Some with murderous intent. How would you feel? That's why there aren't many Obamas in the world, or Trumps, for that matter. The second thing that helped me, was hearing that at the average funeral, at the end of a long life, less than 10 people will cry and mean it, and that the biggest determining factor of attendance at a funeral, is the weather. So here you are, living your life, trying not to upset the apple cart, or rock the boat, and at the end of your life, most of the people you're trying not to upset won't even turn up to say goodbye in case they get their hair wet. Both examples had a massive impact on me.

MOVING FORWARD

The Turtle only moves forward when it sticks its neck out.

Don't wish that what we're discussing here was any different, as Jim Rohn would say; wish that you were better, and work towards it.

I make it an important standard not to get into deep chat about business with close friends and family. I choose not to allow people in my wider circle to remain there if they are against my direction in life, attempt to hold me back, or bring me down. I only follow pages and profiles online that uplift me, inspire me, educate me, or challenge me. If someone is being unnecessarily nasty online, I delete their comment and block them. I like feeling happy. I want to feel good. Life is just too short to allow unnecessary noise in.

This doesn't mean surrounding yourself with yes-men (and women), however. It's important to welcome constructive feedback from voices of experience. I enjoy debating with like minds. I like it when team members throw their hat in the ring and challenge my ideas. When it's with a view on progress, it's important to hear other perspectives.

One of the things I'm most proud of with Property Protege, is the Tribe we've built. Whether in our private online community, our live events, our weekly calls, our get-togethers, or when one member of the Tribe meets another at an entirely separate event, the general attitude and Mindset is first class. Those who are winning, share their stories. Those who are struggling, seek help and always receive it. Those who are active, tap in to share and consume content from like-minded and driven individuals. We have an environment that fosters success, and we have a Tribe of winners. As someone who educates others in Property, I could not ask for more. We are very protective over who gets in, and we are extremely honoured to have those who do. Our people, are awesome.

As we conclude this chapter, I implore you; demand the best for yourself. Set the bar high for who you allow to influence your direction in life. Take pride in being the exception and surround yourself with like-minded souls. As long as you are showing up, doing the right thing, doing good work, and continually learning and growing, then what the naysayers think, is entirely irrelevant and not worth your time or attention.

"It is not the critic who counts; not the man who points out how the strong man stumbles, or where the doer of deeds could have done them better. The credit belongs to the man who is actually in the arena, whose face is marred by dust and sweat and blood; who strives valiantly; who errs, who comes short again and again, because there is no effort without error and shortcoming; but who does actually strive to do the deeds; who knows great enthusiasms, the great devotions; who spends himself in a worthy cause; who at the best knows in the end the triumph of high achievement, and who at the worst, if he fails, at least fails while daring greatly, so that his place shall never be with those cold and timid souls who neither know victory nor defeat." - Theodore Roosevelt

CHAPTER 6:
FINDING THE BELIEF AND CONFIDENCE

Once upon a time, the world was a place of endless possibility. You wanted what you wanted and no one could tell you otherwise. You took chances. You took risks. You rode your bike over the ramp. You climbed the highest trees without a second thought of falling. You jumped off the wall. Your imagination ran wild and life was an epic adventure. But then, something happened. It's something you can see if you watch closely, particularly as children progress through school.

You guessed it. The real world kicked in.

Day by day, slowly but surely, you became a product of your environment. You adopted the beliefs of your parents. You allowed self-doubt to pierce your armour. You listened to the nay-sayers of the world (*also products of their environment*) and you started to believe them. You questioned your abilities. You stopped playing to win, and started playing not to lose. For many people this happens early. For others, it takes a little more time. Sadly, for most, piece by piece, we become a little more cautious in the world, not realising that our doubts are not the products of accurate thinking, but of habitual thinking, fuelled by the world around us, and enforced by repetition of thought.

You were born with a blank slate.

Then, life happened.

On the first couple of days of our Property Protege events, I'm always approached at the breaks by people, looking a little timid. They pull me to the side, and quietly say, *"Paul, what you're sharing is great, but can I tell you my story?"* Whilst I'm respectful enough to listen, the reality is I've heard it all before.

We all have our stories. We all have our past. We all have our baggage. We've all had our challenges. Some people have gone bankrupt. Some have terrible credit. Some have health challenges. Some have failed publicly. Some have gone through hell in their personal lives. I can empathise, and feel for them, but I can't get into the hole of despair with them. I can only reach down and offer a hand to pull them out.

Imagine driving at speed towards your destination, and spending more time looking in the rear view mirror than what's ahead. How far do you think you'd get? The rear view mirror, is for checking behind you, now and then, to learn from whatever's back there, in order to push *forward* on the road ahead. When we focus forward, we can accelerate.

The past is the past. Everything up to this moment, leave it where it is, because no matter your past, you have a spotless future. You have a blank canvas upon which to paint. It's up to you what that looks like.

I believe that most people are living a fraction of their potential. I believe that most people truly want to believe in possibility, in an enhanced quality of life, in increased financial wealth, but something holds them back. It could be fear of success, fear of failure, fear of the unknown, or the power of belief itself. However, I'd be willing to bet that if people truly *knew* that they could achieve whatever it was they wanted to achieve, beyond a shadow of a doubt - it was written, set in stone, and guaranteed - that they would double-down and charge toward it at speed. But it's not written, set in stone, or guaranteed. It is, however, very possible, but reserved only for those who are willing to blend Mindset, knowledge, strategy and action, in the pursuit of what they want.

If people went from believing, to truly knowing, that success was theirs for the taking, most people would leap from their sofa and get to work; but belief, or lack thereof, holds them back. A lack of belief in the process itself, or a lack of belief in themselves.

IF A THING IS POSSIBLE, IT'S WITHIN REACH

On May 6, 1954, Roger Bannister broke the 4-minute-mile. For years, athletes had been striving against the clock, but the elusive 4-minutes had always beaten them. It was as much a psychological barrier as a physical one; an unconquerable mountain. That is, until outlier, iconoclast and lone-wolf Bannister broke through on 3 minutes, 59-and four-tenths of a second. And then, just 46 days after Bannisters feat, Australian runner John Landy, broke the barrier again with a time of 3 minutes 58 seconds. Then, just a year later, 3 more runners broke the barrier in a single race. Over the last half century, more than a thousand runners have conquered a barrier that had once been considered out of reach.

One man went first. He proved the impossible. More followed.

You don't have this problem.

You aren't looking at the example of one man, or a few hundred, or a few thousand. You are looking at the example of 46.8 Million people, who have achieved Millionaire status. 46.8 Million. Let that sink in. And the majority of those people, are first generation rich.

There has never been a more opportune time in history to create wealth. Today, more fortunes are being made than ever, and for good reason. According to Eric Schmidt whilst CEO of Google, *'all information created in human history, is now created every day.'* In the 21st Century, we won't experience 100 years of progress, but 20,000 years of progress equivalent. A child in the middle of the nowhere, has more Global reach with a basic smart phone, than the World Leaders of the late 80's early 90's. We live in a world of rapid change, and every time there's a change in technology, law, social interest, style, the markets, or the latest app or trend, someone gets rich. People become Millionaires by taking advantage of change.

Whilst this is exciting, there's also an air of unpredictability and risk. What's particularly special about Property, is whilst the rest of the world relies on change and emerging markets, Property is, as they say, *'As Safe as Houses.'* Not a lot has changed in terms of approach, which presents a very stable, sober, and proven business to be involved in; but *we* get to benefit from the best of both worlds, in that the tools, resources, applications and technology being made available on a regular basis, have made it even simpler to quicken the pace of progress. Whilst many people will attempt to sell you on the latest Property strategy, the reality is, that many 'new' approaches are either short-term in their life-span and carry unnecessary risk for the get-rich-quick seeker, or they are 'traditional' approaches which have been repackaged and sold under the guise of being new.

Property is not complicated when you know what you're doing. And yet, it can be incredibly unforgiving for those who make mistakes. The most intelligent thing you can do, as we've alluded to throughout, is get your Mindset in check, attain the right knowledge, follow proven strategy, and take the appropriate action, with a support structure in place.

Your goal may not be to become a Millionaire. It may be to create a six-figure income, or a five-figure income, or a few thousand extra each year. Whatever your goal through Property, it has been proven and made possible by thousands upon thousands of others including a great many members of the Tribe at Property Protege, where more wealth is being created and more deals are being done amongst that inner circle, than I've seen anywhere else. If countless others have done it, then it's possible, and if it's possible, it's within reach. So I ask, again, why not you?

It's time to get excited.

Hopefully by this point in the book, you'll have started to see new doors of possibility begin to open up. What's most interesting about this, is that nothing physical has changed. Nothing has changed, yet everything is changing. It's all about the Mindset. It happens internally before it happens externally.

DESTINED FOR GREATNESS

A number of years ago, I ran a podcast called This Week in Property. The podcast is now run by PMW Chief Operating Officer and experienced Property investor Richard Swan, and has grown into something truly special under Richard's stewardship. If you're not already a subscriber, make sure you check it out.

When I led the show, I remember interviewing a Christian Pastor named Jason. Not only was Jason a pastor, but a very successful Entrepreneur. I remember being excited about the interview. I wanted to challenge Jason; not in a negative sense, but in a way that answered my own burning questions. After all, if *it's easier to fit a camel through the eye of a needle than a rich man into heaven*, and *if money is the root of all evil*, I wanted to know how this man could justify his lifestyle, his wealth, and his simultaneous Pastoral role in the Church that he founded. I needed answers.

FINDING THE BELIEF AND CONFIDENCE

Jason held himself well, and to my delight, answered all of my questions in a way that made perfect sense. And, as any good preacher of their faith would do, at the end of the interview, he said, *"Paul, you should come to church. God has a plan for you."* I smiled, *"That's great Jason, but I also have a plan for me."* Feeling I'd gotten the last word, I was taken aback when he continued. *"That's the thing Paul. God's plan for your life, and your own, are one-and-the-same thing. The only obstacle, is you."*

Jason explained that the feeling we wake up with in the morning, that natural drive towards *something*; *is*, the plan for our lives, and it's just as true whatever your faith, religion, or spiritual beliefs. Some people like to paint. Some people like to sing. Some people like to do deals and do business. That feeling that we wake up with in the morning; it's our calling, but more often than not, we silence it, we push it down. It's persistent though. You've felt it many times. It's why, I imagine, you're reading this book.

I don't believe you're here by accident. I believe there's something inside you that's calling you to step forward and pursue what you've always known was yours. I believe in people. I believe we are all destined for our own idea of greatness. If you're reading a book about Property and Business Mindset, then you already know what you have to do.

WHAT YOU FOCUS ON YOU BECOME

In *"Awaken The Giant Within,"* Tony Robbins shares the power of our Reticular Activating System. It sounds complex; and undoubtedly the process is, but the function of your RAS is simple; it determines what you notice and pay attention to. We spend most of our days bombarded with mental and physical stimulus. There are an unlimited number of things we could be paying attention to at a given time, and our conscious mind can only focus on a limited number of those things. Our RAS takes care of this by focusing on more of what's most relevant to us.

Look for what's wrong in the world, and you'll always find it. Keep looking at what's wrong, and it will colour your world and determine how you view life. Conversely, look for what's right in the world, and you'll find that instead. Keep looking, and it too, will colour your world, and determine how you see life. What's wrong is always available. So is what's right. We get more of what we focus on. We become, what we focus on.

If you continually listen to those who tell you it can't be done, soon, if it hasn't already happened, you'll start to believe them. If, however, you continually listen to those who are actively doing what others say can't be done, such as what we see and hear daily in our Property Protege Tribe, soon, you'll start to experience a very different reality.

The more you shift your attention to things that uplift you, inspire you, challenge you, and make you feel good, the more you'll start to gear your mind towards more of the same.

Some people see worthless, empty ground; others see land and development opportunities. Some people see a tired old company, stuck in the past; others see a business that can be brought into the modern world. Some people see a run down Property; others see a development opportunity.

When Property is something you do, you'll have a chance of making it work. When Property is who you are, you'll never have to worry about not being successful. When Business is something you do, you'll have a chance of making it work. When Business is who you are, you'll never have to worry about not being successful.

What you focus on, you get more of. What you focus on, you become.

"We are what we repeatedly do," Aristotle said, "therefore excellence is not an act, but a habit."

PROOF OF CONCEPT

If belief, confidence, or fear, are an issue, I can give you a very simple solution. This same solution will also temper the thoughts, opinions and feelings of those around you. It's very simple; do your first deal. Whether a packaged deal, traded on for a fee, or a buy-to-let, or buy-to-flip. Whatever the approach. Just do it. Do your first deal. Put money on the table. Show yourself that you can do it. Follow a proven system.

My first win was being paid £1,000 for a deal I'd sourced. I wasn't personally in the position to purchase the Property, but at a networking event, an Investor asked me how much I'd take to sell him the opportunity. It was an accidental win. Frankly, I couldn't believe my luck. It didn't feel like £1,000 to me. It felt like a

Million. I'd proven something to myself. I'd found a means to my end, and I went after it aggressively from that point on.

Confidence comes as you move forward. It doesn't happen overnight. We start by borrowing belief by realising the number of people who've been successful before us, in business, and in Property. We look at the number of people around us who are actively doing deals, and who have built their wealth as such. We see that these people are no different from us. They come from all sorts of backgrounds, and all have their stories to tell. We then start to do our own deals, and providing we do not stop, we continue to grow in confidence, to the point that what once scared you, becomes your new version of normal.

Understand that you are nothing more than a handful of comfort zone stretches away from breaking your own barriers. I'm sure you can look back and find things that once frightened you, which are now laughable, almost embarrassing, but now form part of your daily reality. Property is no different. If you've yet to do something, it can be intimidating. Once you do it, and continue doing it, you'll find yourself looking back, a short time from now, and taking pride in who you've become, and what you went through to get there.

CHAPTER 7:
FINDING THE MONEY

Often, I'm asked if it's possible to start in Property without having funds of your own to invest. The answer, is an unequivocal yes. Those who tell you otherwise, either haven't done it, or don't know how. I'm going to handle a few myths in this chapter, and show you just how possible it is to get started, with no money of your own, as many others have.

Whilst having little or no money is the single most common roadblock for those who want to get started in Property, I'd like to put forth that it can actually be an advantage, as we'll discuss later in this chapter. I'd also like to put forth that you don't even have to purchase, or control a Property, to profit from it. Again, which we'll discuss.

What I want you to realise, is that you have options.

The big question that many aspiring investors ask, is *"Can you buy Property with No Money Down?"* Or, better put by various pundits and skeptics, *"Do Unicorns Exist?"* This is one of the most controversial subjects in Property; one I'd like to shed light on.

So what does No Money Down mean?

Back in the day, pre-recession, No Money Down was exactly as it sounds. Not only were you putting No Money Down on Property purchases, you had lenders such as Northern Rock giving 120% Loan to Value; meaning, if a Property was worth £100,000, you'd get the £100,000 and an additional £20,000 over and above. And since many of the Properties were already Walk in Condition, the funds weren't exactly being used to add value.

Today, when people discuss No Money Down, there's an assumption that you're buying Property and that no money is being used in the purchase. This is a misconception. What's generally meant, is that Capital will be employed, just not yours. It could be the banks, a joint venture partner, private investment, commercial lending; in essence, Other Peoples Money, as opposed to No Money Down, and there are many ways this can be done.

STARTING WITH NO MONEY

When I first started in Property, I had no money, no contacts, no resources, and as many would have thought, no chance. It didn't help that I looked like I was 12 years old. There were many things weighed against me, but the way I saw it, I had two choices.

The first choice; don't get started.

The second choice; get resourceful.

From this place, I did two things. The first…

DEAL PACKAGING

I focused on Deal Packaging, or Property Trading as it's sometimes known. I would source deals, preferably Below Market Value, and even better, where value could be added. I would run the numbers, negotiate with sellers, structure the deal, arrange the finance, lock the deal down, and pull the relevant third parties together. I would sit in the middle, and without owning the Properties or being part of the upside, would make upwards of £5,000 per Property trade, selling (trading) deals to Investors. When I learned how to appropriately monetise the process, this rose to between £7,500 and £10,000 average per trade.

I taught myself how to make money from Property, without owning Property, and without the requirement for personal capital, and none of it was particularly difficult. There we no gimmicky strategies or cleverly named approaches. It was pure and simple buy-to-let and buy-to-flip, but rather than being the buyer, I was the finder.

The interesting thing is, I *still* cover this strategy at Property Protege to this day. Why? Because this approach helped me understand the game at a deeper level. It helped me build my network. It helped me generate cash flow. I was providing a valuable service to those with no time or inclination to source deals through Direct to Vendor marketing. I had something people wanted, and I capitalised on the opportunity. That same opportunity still exists as it did when I started, and is a great place for those without capital to start.

The second thing I focused on...

JOINT VENTURES

Sometimes, I'd come across a deal where I thought, *"This is too good to sell."* The only problem, however, was that I still had no personal funds to invest, let alone cover the refurb, associated legal fees, void periods, and so on.

So again, I got resourceful. I developed a Mindset that said 'having 50% of something is better than 100% of nothing,' so began to look for Joint Venture partners who could cover the acquisition and other associated costs.

Let's say there was a deal I wanted for myself, but £40,000 was required, which would cover both the deposit and the refurb. At this point, I'd pull in a Joint Venture partner. *They* would cover the cost, *we* would get the mortgage, and the lender would cover the balance. We'd be 50/50 partners on the deal and would split the rental income. After 'buying right' in the first place, based on strong investment criteria, preferably at a price below market value, and adding additional value, we would refinance the Property, which would pay back the initial investment, and allow us to split the remaining profit. I would then own 50% of a Property, and benefit from 50% of the profit, without having put a single penny into the deal.

So why would someone want to do this with you? I have a better question, why wouldn't they? You're the one with the deal. You've done the leg work. You have the goods. Most people think that the person with the money holds the cards and calls the shots. This is far from the truth. There's a frightening amount of available capital out there. If you have a deal, and you've structured it, locked it down, and pulled the various moving parts into place; you'll have friends, family members, Investors, and others with available capital seeking to Joint Venture with you.

This is how I started to build my personal Portfolio; and when I maxed out my ability to obtain mortgages, I began using legal contracts and shareholding agreements to secure my interests.

I took a similar approach with flips, but instead of splitting rental profits, we'd pay back the initial investment upon selling the Property, and split the remaining profit.

Now let's go a step further.

Frankly, I began to realise that 50/50 wasn't working for me. Why should it be 50/50? After all, I was doing all the work, whilst my Joint Ventures partners contributed nothing more than the Capital. Surely, a Joint Venture agreement didn't always have to be split down the middle? Surely I could still go in on a deal with someone, and offer a percentage return on Investment, either per annum or per deal? And surely I could make money throughout the entire process, including the back end?

Whether you're packaging and selling a deal, or Joint Venturing with a 50/50 partner, or Joint Venturing with a lesser percentage silent partner, there are many ways to produce additional revenue. This is something we focus heavily on at

Property Protege. You don't know what you don't know, and when you start to learn what's truly possible, it opens up a whole new world of potential and opportunity for long and short term wins.

INVESTOR FUNDING

Another way of operating without using your own capital, similar to working with Joint Venture partners, is to raise finance. After doing countless Joint Ventures in the early days, I started to think, *'What if I could raise £100,000 or more from a collective, and rather than taking them into a specific Property deal, I could offer a percentage return?"*

At first this was a scary thought, but as I was entirely confident in my abilities and had the experience and track record to back it up, I found it fairly straightforward to raise the funds, over and over again; *always* delivering on what was promised.

Why would anyone want to do this?

Let's imagine a friend or family member has £100,000 equity in their home. You help them understand that their funds aren't working for them, and educate them on how they could be. Following your guidance, they release the equity, which costs them 1.5-3%, which to me, spells 'cheap borrowings.' They give you the £100,000, and you put the funds to work for a percentage return. Let's say the return was 10% over the year. That's 7% after paying back the 3% cost of borrowing. Now, they've taken money from their home that was sitting idle, put it to work, and it's providing a return, which they can choose to enjoy, or roll back in for another round. They're making money, you're making money, and everyone is happy.

There's an abundance of capital out there, burning holes in peoples pockets, tied up in their homes, or sitting in an ISA for a whopping 1% if they're lucky. We're talking here about friends, family members, colleagues, and what we call 'Preferred Investors.' A Preferred Investor is not a Property Investor. Property Investors can be some of the most difficult people to deal with, as their expectations are higher. Preferred Investors are simply individuals with Capital, whom you'd come into contact with through your network, through networking, or through social media, perhaps. Again, we cover this, and much more at Property Protege. What's important to keep in mind for now, is that there's no shortage of funding from individuals. It's out there in abundance; you just need the goods to back it up.

COMMERCIAL LENDING

And then there's Commercial Lending; another angle you can play to purchase Property without your own personal funds. Some lenders will offer you 100% of the purchase costs, 100% of the development finance, and they'll also cover your fees. Sounds like a dream come true, but it may not always be the best option as the cost of finance will be significantly more expense. That being said, it's all relative. If you have no funds for your deal in the first place, then you're coming out on top regardless.

A commercial lender will most likely look for a track record, which could be a previous deal or development. If you have no track record, then you could gain one in the eyes of the lender, by partnering with others who do.

A lender will want to know if there's any security. Well, they'll likely be taking first charge security over the asset that you're purchasing, and if you're buying at the right price, and adding substantial value, then they will see this in their appraisal, understand their risk, and determine whether they want to give you funding for the project. If the numbers work, they'll most likely want to give it to you. A lender may also need additional security, such as a second charge on other assets, such as your own home, which of course you'll be comfortable doing, because you've worked the numbers, mitigated the risk through your due diligence, and understand that the uplift outweighs anything else, so you'll go ahead and do the deal. To be frank, some lenders aren't even concerned about your income or credit; they're looking at the deal and your ability to see it through.

MAKING IT HAPPEN

No Money Down is a controversial discussion, but it doesn't have to be. When we move past the play on words, we realise that Investors discussing No Money Down, aren't necessarily suggesting that no funds have been used, just that they haven't leveraged their own funds.

Unicorns do exist, just not in the way that people think.

Of course there are others who'll tell you that you can in fact *purchase* Property with no funds leveraged whatsoever, which is nonsense. To *'purchase'* is to *'acquire by paying.'* What's really being suggested, is *'controlling'* Property, as opposed to purchasing. This isn't a bad thing. There are ways and means, but it's *not* No Money Down. Again, it's all semantics. What matters most as we come to the end of this chapter, is that you start to realise that you can in fact get your start or accelerate in Property without funds.

I mentioned earlier that it may even be an advantage to start without funds. Quite simply, if 'person A' and 'person B' start at the same time; 'person A' having £100,000 to invest, and 'person B' having nothing; 'person B' has a distinct advantage, in that from the word GO they must learn to raise finance. Once 'person A' has put their funds to work, they'll find themselves in the same position as 'person B' started, with no funds to invest. 'Person B' has the head start, even though it looked like 'person A' had the advantage.

We have countless options available to us in Property. Whilst some see black and white, and only know what they know, others are seekers of truth and information, finding whole new worlds of possibility and opportunity opening up to them. The most important thing you can do, is get educated on the specifics of putting what we've discussed to work, as well as learning creative strategies and approaches to accelerating in the game. What we've discussed here is barely even the tip of the iceberg. Now that your Mindset is in check with this particular aspect, and you're beginning to see what's behind the curtain, have a look into Property Protege and find out more about how we can support you.

PROPERTY SUCCESS MINDSET

CHAPTER 8:
FINDING THE DEALS

I knocked on the door, a little nervous. My friend, who stood by my side, had convinced me that we should at least give it a go. Five minutes earlier, we'd been driving past an estate that, at the time, played host to my dream home, a four story Townhouse. Now, I was standing at the front door of one of two houses with a For Sale post at the front.

The door opened.

"Sorry to bother you. I'm looking to buy in the area, and I've noticed your For Sale sign has been up for some time. Would you be interested in discussing a private sale?"

The door closed.

Ok. Back in the car.

"Let's do one more," my friend said. Ok. Reluctantly, I went to the next door. I knocked. A few moments later, an irate women, around five foot tall, pulled the door open. "What?" She said. Not off to a great start. I repeated my statement. "Sorry to bother you.

I'm looking to buy in the area, and I've noticed your For Sale sign has been up for some time. Would you be interested in discussing a private sale?"

"Come in," she said, beckoning us inside.

She apologised for her initial opening. It turned out her best friend was in labour on the top floor of the house, and things were a little up-in-the-air. However, as it happened, she was more than happy to receive us. She showed us around the house, from the Cinema room on the bottom floor, to the bedrooms on the top. As it happened, she and her husband had been attempting to sell the Property for some time, but it just wasn't selling. Her husband worked offshore, and they were desperate to move closer to family. I had a good chat with her, and a few weeks later, met with her husband upon his return.

I moved into that house a month later.

It was the second door we knocked. I found a seller, motivated to sell to me, on a structured arrangement, and I personally lived in that house for 5 years.

The reason I'm telling you this story, is because purchasing Property at a price below market value, and finding deals where others are not looking, and the sheer potential of the opportunity in front of you, is absolutely frightening. Let's dig in.

WHERE DO MOST PEOPLE LOOK FOR DEALS?

If you're new to Property, you'll have read the word "Deal" countless times in this book now, but like many people, if you do not know where to find them, it can seem a far fetched idea. Another Unicorn, even. Even to many who are already operating in Property, whose limited knowledge of sourcing deals holds them back from achieving their true potential.

If you can't find the deals, you can't get the money.

So where do most people look? Conventional thinking would point you towards the two primary sources commonly understood in Property; estate agents, and RightMove. There is, however, an inherent challenge in both, in that it's what everyone else is doing, also.

Let's start with Estate Agents. This is where I began. Looking like I was 12 years old, I'd meet with Estate Agents in the hope of building lasting relationships where I'd be passed deals as a preferred buyer. Of course, I wasn't the first person to walk through their door hoping to get lucky, there were countless others like me. I also knew it was a long term play, and that winning favour, over anyone else on the books, was going to take time and effort. I had no other way of finding deals at the time, so I put in the hard yards.

Note the word 'deals.' We're not talking about Properties selling at full market value. We're talking about Properties that must sell fast, below the market value, and preferably where substantial value can be added. There's high demand for such deals, and even back then, before the number of Property Investors had blown up, it was still very rare that I'd ever see a deal thrown my way; and if I said no, I was unlikely to be thrown another.

In today's market, Estate Agents have seen enough Tyre Kickers come and go, wasting their time. There's an impatience, even an arrogance towards Investors. The problem, is that with apparent limited options, building relationships with Estate Agents is the first go-to solution for new and aspiring Investors. It's very crowded indeed.

And then there's RightMove, which of course, also requires agents in many cases. RightMove can be a phenomenal tool for sourcing if you have an eye for the detail. At Property Protege we spend some time going through RightMove, looking for Properties that require work, or where additional value can be added through extensions, adding rooms, and so on. When you know what you're looking for, you will find potential deals. But then, you run into similar problems. You're up against every other Investor out there.

WHERE THE PROFESSIONALS OPERATE

And then there are a rare breed of people that know how to do this properly. Generally, because they've worked with us on Property Protege and we've shown them how. Whilst Estate Agents and RightMove are viable strategies where the occasional win may take place, there's another route that opens the floodgates of opportunity, and presents a very unique opportunity indeed. That route, is called Direct to Vendor marketing.

To understand this approach, you must first understand who your market is. The two words to become familiar with, are Motivated Sellers. A Motivated Seller is someone who is motivated to sell their Property, and is willing to entertain reasonable offers from prospective buyers. They generally do not have the luxury of time to list and sell on the open market, and for a variety of reasons, the sale of their Property will generally solve other problems, hence the initial motivation.

Who are these people? They're regular people, from all walks of life.

In many cases, Motivated Sellers are financially motivated. They've found themselves in a position where their Property is no longer the family home, but an asset that can be sold to solve urgent financial problems. Someone loses their job, or someone goes bankrupt, or someone is up to their eyes in pressing debt. Perhaps they don't have savings and have no way out of a difficult situation. Let's be straight here; many people have been in situations where finances are extremely tight. Some people, such as the Motivated Sellers being discussed, have been tipped just that little bit further, and are in need of a fast solution.

Other people sell for a variety of reasons, including but not limited to; facing repossession, requiring a discreet sale, properties in dire need of repair, going through divorce or separation, bereavement, behind on payments, emigrating, broken chains, and so on. It's a horrible thing to find yourself, or another, in a situation like this, but it's a harsh reality in life. It happened, and now you, the Investor, get to help them out of it.

Notice the word 'help.' I must stress, that you have a responsibility to help people. This is not about taking advantage. This is about using your knowledge and skillset to provide a solution for someone in a difficult situation. I remember being asked if I felt bad about profiting from other peoples misery, but in reality, when a seller gives you a hug and thanks you profusely for what you've done; and when this happens time and time again, you know you're doing some good in the world, whilst building your business on the back of it.

WHERE DO WE FIND THEM?

If sellers are normal people, and they're everywhere, how exactly do we know which people are in need of our help? How do we find them? This is where we put on our marketing hats. Property, as a business, is about more than investing in deals. It's a business, and businesses have various moving parts. When you first get started, you're the janitor and the CEO. When you start to get moving, you slowly begin to build a team around you that can handle tasks, freeing you to focus on your core strengths. One of those strengths, must be an understanding of marketing. Even if you have a marketing team, you are still the Director, the Conductor, the Operator; the person with the big picture. However you want to put it, you're the head honcho, and you know the desired outcomes. With this in mind, you are a marketer first, before all else. Own this. It's a vital role. Leads and deals are the lifeblood of your business. No leads, no deals; no business.

In order to source Properties from Motivated Sellers, you must first seek to understand the location you wish to target. This can be your own locale, or another, and is known as your Goldmine area. You must understand this area inside out. You must understand the local market inside out. You must understand values. You must build your local network with builders and other members of your Power Team. You must spend time studying the lay of the land; pricing, recent sales, rental figures, and so on.

When you know your Goldmine area, and you're ready to start marketing, you simply *cast a wide net, in a small area.* Meaning, you launch a strategic marketing campaign with the intent to dominate the local area. When you're doing your local Goldmine area marketing, you want to be everywhere, in all places, at all times. A study by Forbes concluded that people are exposed to 4,000 to 10,000 ads each day. What that means for us, is that we have unlimited ways to market to, and get the attention of, our target market. We must make the leap from consumer, to producer. Be everywhere. Have your leaflets in pubs, clubs, takeaways, restaurants, local services, and most importantly, through people's front doors. Put bandit boards around the local area. Rent space on billboards. Use print media, radio, and direct mail. Knock doors. Build relationships with local professionals, debt advisory services, divorce lawyers, citizens advice bureaus. Run Google PPC campaigns driving traffic to your website. Run Facebook ads to your website. Retarget all website visitors by following them around online.

Everywhere, anywhere, always.

It's important to note that you must have a strong sourcing website. Companies without an online presence aren't taken seriously. If you're in the market to purchase Property, even to source Properties to bridge the gap between buyer and seller, you must have a professional online presence. Your website must be the central point of all of your marketing. All roads lead there. It must be professionally designed, it must work across all platforms, it must be well structured with strong copy, and it must serve one singular purpose; to convert viewers into leads. A great resource for this, and various other marketing tools, can be found at PropertySourcingSolutions.com

By being all places at all times, in your local Goldmine area, you'll be hard to miss. You'll build trust through longevity and awareness. You'll start to be noticed. You'll become the local go-to guy-or-girl in your area, as I did, and you'll dominate your space.

THE AGGRESSIVE PURSUIT

When I first began sourcing Property off-market, I became overwhelmed with the number of leads that came in. I don't do anything by halves. I am aggressive in my approach. If something is to be done, it's to be done right. If there's a market out there for what I have to offer, you can bet that I'll go after it hard, until I get what I'm looking for. I took the approach suggested above, and was literally all places at all times. The business started to come slowly at first, but with repetition and continued marketing, I began to receive lead after lead through my websites. It was a busy time. I basically sat in my small home, the first Property purchase I'd made, and spent minute after minute on the phone. This is the first time I started to make real money in Property, and it was all through packaging and trading deals. That's how I got my start. Find the deals, sell them on, and repeat. As more deals completed, I started enjoying my money, working with Joint Venture partners, and in time, rolling my collected funds into deals.

DEALS ARE EVERYWHERE

If you start looking for deals, you're going to find them. Part of this involves knowing what a deal looks like, and part of this is knowing how to find them. It's not rocket science, and it's not difficult, but it does require knowledge and a level of experience. We can help you with this at Property Protege. At the 3-day Intensive, and for the 12-months support period that follows, we provide full training on deal sourcing. There is no reason why you would not and could not source deals. Of course you could take what's been said above and get going without our support, but why climb Everest alone, when you can have a guide who's walked the path, knows the pitfalls, knows what to do, and what not to do, to ensure you make it the top.

Deals are everywhere. The longer you're in the game, the more business you're going to produce without even having to market. People are going to know who you are. Word will spread. Clients you've helped through ethical trading will pass referral business. You'll turn away more than you take on. Sound good? Excellent. Now that we've worked on the possibility aspect of Mindset on the sourcing front, let's move onto our next subject.

CHAPTER 9:
FINDING THE TIME

Around the time my second daughter, Hannah, came into the world, I had a chat with my life long best friend Billy about adjusting to the change. I've always been highly productive, and part of the reason for that, is by seeking out the best advice.

You see, Billy has four daughters; 2, 4, 6, and 8. He's a loving and connected father and husband, an active Biker, a businessman who owns and controls multiple companies, including owning substantial shares in my own, he trains daily for strength, and has a very active life. Yet every time I speak to Billy, he seems to have it altogether. He has balance in his life, and is constantly expanding on all fronts.

When I spoke with Billy about adjusting to new routines, he told me, "Paul. When my first daughter was born, it was a challenge. When my second daughter was born, we realised one had been easy. When my third daughter was born, we realised two had been easy. When my fourth daughter was born, we realised three had been easy. Every time you step into a new challenge, you can either back down or get stronger. You can raise your capacity to handle more, or you can buckle and throw in the towel."

If you think back to the Wealth Thermostat from chapter 2, it's the same conversation. You can either live at your current version of normal, or you can raise your game. The version of you that takes home £50,000 per annum, is very different from the version of you that takes home £500,000 per annum. Similarly, the version of you that is able to adjust your use of time and get personal and professional leverage to produce £50,000 per annum, is very different from the version of you that is able to adjust your use of time and get personal and professional leverage to produce £500,000 per annum.

Time is the one thing we all have in common. Whether you're Richard Branson, or Branson Richards, we all have 1,440 minutes in a day. How you use them, is an entirely different story, and how you *get leverage*, is another story still.

WE ALL HAVE THE TIME

Here's the reality. Limited time has never stopped a person who was truly committed to an outcome, but provides an excellent excuse for the person who was not up to the challenge in the first place. If you want something, then it's generally not that time does not exist to make it happen, but that your use of time and prioritisation requires adjustment.

As Seneca said almost 2000 years ago, "It is not that we have a short time to live, but that we waste a lot of it. Life is long enough, and a sufficiently generous amount has been given to use for the highest achievements, if it were all well invested."

He also went on to say, "People are frugal in guarding their personal Property, but as soon as it comes to squandering time, they are most wasteful of the one thing in which it is right to be stingy. I would like to fasten on someone from the older generation and say to him, 'I see that you have come to the last stage of human life; you are close upon your hundredth year; come now, hold an audit of your life. Reckon how much of your time has been taken up by a money-lender, how much by a mistress, a patron, a client, quarrelling with your wife, punishing your servants, dashing around on your social obligations."

Different times. Same idea.

Time exists, but priorities must change.

I always find it interesting when someone tells me that time is a challenge, but they manage to find the time to catch the latest news, play 5-a-side football midweek, watch their favourite shows on Netflix, spend the weekend drinking, and so on. They say that they don't have time, but a quick glance at their social media suggests otherwise.

Of course, some folk genuinely feel completely overwhelmed and life has presented challenges which seem to squeeze every ounce of energy and time from them. I get that. But still, I'd argue that time can be found somewhere, somehow.

Get up an hour earlier, cut tasks that no longer serve you, order your food shop online, purchase goods from Amazon, stop watching the news, stop reading tabloids, distance yourself from time wasters, limit time on social media, eat higher quality foods and exercise in order to create energy and focus, lower alcohol consumption, outsource personal tasks, hire people to fill roles that generally consume your time, systemise your daily to-do's to create simplicity.

Here's a shocker for you. If you were able to create one hour per day, each day for one year, that single hour, over the year, would add up to 9 40-hour workweeks of time. If I told you, that you had 9 40-hour workweeks of time to build something with your life, do you feel this would be sufficient, providing relevant focus and prioritisation was in place? There's no arguing with this. And what if you could create two hours, or more?

Whatever you're going through, understand that others have likely gone through the same or worse, and come out on top regardless. Expanding your capacity is a choice. There's always time if you're willing to be honest with yourself, and actively look for it.

WE MUST TAKE CONTROL

The average lifespan is 78 years. That's 683,280 hours. The average person sleeps 8 hours per night, totalling 227,760 hours of life asleep. The average person working 9 to 5, from 18 to 68 years old, 253 days per annum, works 101,200 hours, and spends an average of 18,975 hours travelling to and from work. The average person spends 195 days per annum at school, for a total of 6.5 hours, for a minimum of 11 years, totalling 13,942 hours, with an additional average of 2,145 hours spent travelling to and from school.

If you think about it, that's more than 54% of your life accounted for, before even take basic essentials such as eating, visiting the bathroom, washing, dressing; much less social media, holidays, birthdays, nights out, dating, and other regular tasks and activities.

We can't cut down the school time, nor the sleep, but we can certainly cut into the 120,000 hours plus, that goes into employment; making other people wealthy. If we diligently pursue increased productivity, we can create additional time through leverage, and we can cut back on what matters least, replaced by what matters most.

One of the biggest challenges in the modern world is technology and digital distraction. If you have an iPhone, look at your Screen Time. Look at your call time. Use apps such as RescueTime to track the amount of time spent on social networks and elsewhere. Digital distraction feels good, and it's easy, but it's the path to nowhere. If you look at my phone, you'll see no notifications. Nor will you hear it ring. Nor will you sense it vibrate. Nor will you see little red circles with white numbers on my apps. I've turned it all off. Why? Because I'll get to these things when it suits me, not when it suits others. Your phone should be an asset, a tool for leverage. It should not control you.

GET LEVERAGE AND FOCUS

I once heard it said, that it's better to be World Class at a few things, than mediocre at many; that Super Achievers are generally World Class at their 'vital few,' whilst being fairly average at most other things. So the first question is, *'What matters most to you in life?'* And the second question, *'What are you willing to give up to get what you really want?'*

Obvious options include television, news, sports, music, and social media. Committing an entire day to the success of a football match, only to forget the score a few weeks later, is a great pastime, and there's nothing wrong with doing it, but if we come back to our core questions of *'what matters most'* and *'what are you willing to give up,'* you can begin to form ideas around what you can drop entirely, and what you can slow to moderation.

When you've created space for what's most important, then your focus turns to PROGRESS and EXPANSION in those areas. For me, my focus is my health, my wife, my children, my business, and my own personal and professional growth. And in each of those areas, I have a deeper purpose and focus. Based on what you choose to make important, you can then identify your vital few strategic priorities, and aggressively move forward.

If you're unclear on what your professional strategic priorities should be in Property, they depend on a number of things, including your desired outcomes, chosen strategies and approach. Of course, we go much deeper on this at Property Protege.

The most important choice you have to make at any given moment, is what you choose to make important. When you know what matters most, my advice, is that you outsource everything else where possible. In your personal life; cleaning, ironing, gardening, maintenance, painting, decorating, car valets, and whatever else possible. In your professional life, anything that can be passed to others at a lower rate than what you're able to produce by having your focus on what matters most. First, most likely through outsourcing, and when the time is right later, building a team.

TAKE IT AT YOUR OWN PACE

Every now and then someone in our Property Protege Tribe will tell me they feel like they're behind their peers in terms of progress. What's interesting, is that no one is behind anything or anyone. If it takes a day, a week, a month, or a year, you go at a pace that makes sense to YOU. You are the only benchmark. You are the only competition.

Remember, success is subjective. It's a personal experience based on how you define what success is to you, the timeframe you wish to achieve your various targets in, and the approach you're going to take to get there. At Property Protege, we provide the education, the tools, the resources, and the support, but beyond that, it's up to the individual to do what's right for them, and to choose the pace that they feel comfortable with.

It's also important to enjoy the process. To 10X constantly, is to burn out. You can get started in Property in your spare time. If you don't have spare time, you can create it. When you get moving, you must remember to balance the other important aspects of your life, as opposed to being one-dimensionally business-focused, whilst neglecting family, health and wellness. Life is for living, and living is about more than just business.

However long it takes, I want you to get there. My focus isn't on you getting rich quick, it's on long term sustainable success that lasts a lifetime. It's about helping you become the person you have to become, armed with the tools, resources, knowledge and support, to get to work in Property and create the life you've always known you were meant to live.

CHAPTER 10:
FINDING THE RIGHT INFORMATION AND SUPPORT

"Get it right in Property, and you may do very well. Get it wrong, however, even just once, and it can spell disaster that you may never recover from." The short and direct words of a successful Businessman who'd taken a moment of his time to pass on this - and only this - wisdom. The memory of his words echoed in my ear, as my heart pounded. I was in the thick of my first deal, and it wasn't going well.

I was 21 years old, completely naive, and was following the conflicting advice of a number of people, all of whom I'd *thought* were successful in Property.

I thought I'd nailed it. I'd negotiated 20% off the market value for *(what would be)* a buy-to-let, and had been led to believe that if I managed to get this discount, I wouldn't have to pay a deposit, which of course, looking back, is ridiculous. I was feeling quite proud of myself, when, on a Monday morning, the solicitor phoned me. "Paul, completion will take place this coming Friday. You'll have to transfer the £13,800." I calmly replied, *"No, it's fine, I don't need to send any money because I'm doing a No Money*

Down deal. The mortgage broker has arranged the mortgage. He's taking care of all of that. I'm not putting money in." The solicitor asked me to explain how this was a No Money Down deal, which I did. He replied, *"Paul, son, that's not how this deal is structured and it's not how it's going to go through. You need to come up with the money. Are you able to do that?"*

"Yes, of course." I replied.

"Good," he said, "Because you've concluded contracts, which means you are legally obliged to purchase the Property."

I felt my stomach turn, as I put the phone down, and thought, *"That's it, I'm completely screwed."* I was in my early 20's, remember. I felt like it was game over. I was completely ignorant, had no one to guide me, was overwhelmed, and frankly, a little terrified.

I phoned the mortgage broker. Too little too late. I phoned the seller. Too late on that front, also. I approached the handful of people in my social circle whom I believed may have been able to help me. It wasn't happening. Thankfully, at the eleventh hour, my *then* partners dad offered to put some money in, as did a person I'd met on holiday a few years earlier who happened to be a business owner and had taken a shine to me. I increased my overdraft on two accounts to bring up the balance, and managed to take it over the line.

I still own this Property, over a decade later. It generates great cash flow, and has increased in value over time, through Capital Growth, and was renovated several years in.

But it could have gone very differently.

Poor advice, conflicting information, lack of knowledge and education, and no support, almost took me out of the game on my first round.

I wasn't prepared to let that happen again.

I made the decision to get educated.

I found the best, did my homework, and paid them.

THE NEED FOR RELEVANT & QUALITY INFORMATION

Despite more information being readily available to us at the click of a button than at any point in history; as a species, we've never been more overweight, unhealthy, depressed, struggling, and unhappy than we are now.

If more information was the answer, we'd live in a different world.

Take Property specifically. Online and offline, there are forums, groups, communities, blogs, podcasts, YouTube channels, books, seminars, networking events, gatherings, events, conferences and more. Yet more often than not, you'll find yourself drowning in a murky sea of information, thick with conflicting advice. Search, for example, various Property forums online. One forum will slate the leadership of the other, and vice versa. Look at some of the most popular Facebook groups discussing Property. One person says black, the other says white. Both stand by their opinions. Unfortunately, whilst many will tell you that everything you need to know is available for free online, it's piecing it together, knowing who's right, wrong, experienced and otherwise, that presents the problem.

Frankly, many of the people who tell you that everything you need is free online, simply haven't achieved a respectable level of success in Property, and are giving you potentially dangerous advice, sending you into no man's land without a map or support.

There are some, however, who *have* been successful, who'll tell you the same thing; but in this rare exception of cases, such people may have forgotten the obstacles and time it took for them to achieve the level of success they now enjoy, and despite their best intentions, unless they're willing to hold your hand and help you avoid the many pitfalls and ever increasing levels of conflicting information; they too, risk giving you potentially dangerous advice by suggesting you go-it alone. Whilst Property will take time and should 'by no means' be considered a means to get rich quick, it also doesn't have to take forever, and better to get help, support, and a clear roadmap, than to fumble in the dark.

I like to think of the world of information like a jigsaw puzzle. Sure, you can gather lots of pieces online. However, some of the pieces you'll gather aren't for the specific puzzle you're attempting to piece together, even though they may appear to be so. You'll also be hard pushed to finish your 10,000-piece puzzle, without a BOX with THE BIG PICTURE.

Property Education fast tracks the process, giving you the pieces, the box, and a helping hand to ensure you complete the challenge successfully.

THE PROPERTY EDUCATION INDUSTRY

On the flip side, there are those who aren't fans of Property Education. It may surprise you to know that I, as a Property Educator, resonate with many of them.

In an unregulated space such as Property Education, it can be difficult knowing who to trust. Frankly, long before anyone else would ask the question, *"Who is Paul McFadden to teach others about Property?"* I asked myself the same thing and laboured over the point.

"Who was I to teach this?" After all, I'd made some big mistakes. My first deal almost took me out of the game. My back has been against the wall more times than I can remember. I've found myself in terrible debt. I've been screwed over. I've chosen the wrong partners and backed the wrong horses. Every mistake you can think of, I've made it.

So who was I to teach Property?

I was EXACTLY what was required. Because, whilst making many mistakes, as people do, I LEARNED FROM THEM, and made them only once. I'd also flipped numerous Properties, built a substantial personal portfolio, Joint Ventured with many of the best and brightest, and was a rising name in the circuit. Long before I taught others, I'd achieved a respectable level of success, and had gone on to set up the UK's second largest Property Networking Event in January 2010. I saw what was going on in the industry, and I believed I could do better. I knew I'd make money as an educator, and I knew it would be fun, but my driving force was the ability to find good people, help them, and work with them.

So when I see opportunists pop up after doing a deal or two, with more marketing savvy than Property experience, muddying the waters in a game that I'm passionate about, it leaves a bitter taste in my mouth. Some people see Property Education as a means to make money and nothing more. That doesn't sit right with me. There are also others who've been in the game far longer than I have, but who've dropped the ball in supporting their clients, who continue to make notable errors in judgement, who've publicly let down investors, or made irreparable mistakes. I don't make it my business to criticise or take a stance on the actions or inactions of others, but it's an issue, and one I'd be wrong not to acknowledge.

That's not to suggest that Property Protege and what we do at PMW is the only route. There are many great training companies in the industry and many good, experienced, knowledgable people who deliver education. The training industry is just like any other.

Good mechanics, not-so-good mechanics. Good personal trainers, not-so-good personal trainers. Good therapists, not-so-good therapists. Good Property Education companies, and, well, you get the idea.

With such a substantial upside and so much to gain, I want to take the remainder of this chapter to highlight what you should be looking for from an Education company, to ensure it's an experience that catapults you forward, and helps you create wealth for a lifetime.

CHOOSING A PROPERTY EDUCATION COMPANY

Whether through my own company, or another, here's what you should look for.

Select a training company with a long term focus on results. The reality is, it's not going to happen overnight. There is no magic pill in Property. There is no secret formula. There's simply right Mindset, right knowledge, right strategy, and right action. Accompany this with consistency over time, a commitment to continued personal growth, and strong support system; and you have a recipe for success in Property.

Select a training company with depth of training. When working with a Property Education company, make sure that what you're going to learn will be taught in a manner that is easy to understand, broken down, and simplified. It's no fun to be either underwhelmed at an event packed with fluff and space-filler content, or overwhelmed with a fire-hose of content that is impossible to consume, understand, or keep up with. A look at feedback videos from other clients who've attended the same event will help.

Select a training company where you know what you're getting, and you're not required to pay more to receive what you thought you were getting. There's nothing wrong with being offered additional services, but to turn up to an event expecting to learn about a specific strategy or concept, only to realise that you'll have to pay more to get the real information, can be a painful reality, leaving you out of pocket, and let down.

Select a training company with ongoing and unparalleled support. This is essential. You can spend a few days learning and consuming content, but the real learning starts when you go back into the world and put theory into practice. This is when you find yourself with questions. This is when you run into obstacles. This is when you need the guiding hand of experience to help steer you through. This, is one of the most important aspects of selecting a Property Education company, and cannot be overstated.

Select a training company with a community at its heart. Just as help and support from an Education company is essential, it's equally important to work with a company with community at its heart. A strong network of like-minded individuals, on the same journey, with varying degrees of experience and success, all working together to support one another; sharing wins, sharing lessons learned, and propelling all-involved forward.

Select a training company with a track record in client wins. Before working with a Property Education company, ensure that there are more than a few client case studies and clear wins on display. Written testimonials can be fabricated. It can and does happen. Look for video based testimony, where stories are shared and wins are detailed. Not everyone is active online, but it can help to find such people on social media to see if they are in fact active in Property, as opposed to having been paid or coerced into providing feedback.

Select a training company that don't give you the hard sell. I don't see the need for it. High pressure in any industry is wrong, and generally leaves people with buyers remorse, or worse, justifying their decisions to themselves and those around them. If value is clear, your decision will be easy. Doing your homework upfront will paint that picture of value.

Select a training company that doesn't sugarcoat or tell you what you want to hear. Let's be honest, there's enough bullshit out there. Whenever a company tells you they're the best in the world, or can make you an overnight success, or can make you a Millionaire in 90-days, it's most likely bullshit. Whilst it's important to realise that many things you've yet to experience are in fact possible, it's just as important to see the clear and obvious bullshit when it's right in front of you. It's not difficult to detect.

It's important to do your homework.

The points above will assist you in making your decision.

PROPERTY PROTEGE ® AND PMW

I felt it appropriate to advise on what to look for when selecting a Property Education company, as not everyone will resonate with me or my message. That's ok. Whether it's PMW or an entirely different company, I would encourage you to find a good reputable Property Education company who tick all the right boxes, and start learning. Simplify, get the right knowledge, learn the right strategies, and work with the right people who will support you, allowing you to progress and expand in the world of Property.

With that being said, I categorically WANT your business.

Providing it's the right fit for you and for us, I wouldn't be serving you if I didn't highlight that the criteria above derives from our standards as a training company.

For years, we've made it an absolute commitment to be the very best in what we do. Not in comparison to others, but by holding a mirror up to what we do, how we do it, and the impact it has on those whom we're grateful to call our clients; our Tribe. Our focus is not on bringing you in and pushing you out, but on your long-term success. We don't do one-night stands. We're in it for the long haul. Our training is deep and focused, and every person in attendance is catered for, attended to, supported at our events, and supported thereafter. We make it crystal clear what you're getting, and whilst from time to time we may make additional training available to you, it's complimentary in nature, as opposed to taking away from the programme you've paid to attend. Our support is second to none. We support you at the event. We support you in our group. We answer every question thrown at us. We spend time with all involved on a weekly group zoom call. We've got your back for the 12-month duration of the programme. Not only do we support you, but our Tribe are hard wired to look after one another. We're selective and protective over our community, and want as many people involved as possible to help and support other members. We don't sugarcoat, we don't hard sell, and there are over 200 client videos on our website, with some being over an hour in length, packed with information that can help before you've even joined us.

Is that enough?

Hey, if you want more, there's no shortage of information on my podcast, on my YouTube channel, and on my social media. If you're not quite ready to take the leap into training, you can at least start learning the basics from the sidelines. And when you're ready to kick start your Property journey and get going, we'll be here for you.

At Property Protege, there's no reason why anyone involved cannot be successful, whatever success may mean to them. The training, the resources, the support; all provided in abundance. You'll be hard pushed to find negativity from our clients online, and whilst we have no intention on being the biggest, we are completely focused on being the best we can be for you. That's it. No hard sell. If you want to know more, go to PropertyProtege.com and book a call with our team. They'll have a friendly chat to find out what you want, and to ensure that it's the right fit for you and for us. If everyone is happy, we'll move forward.

I'll add additional information about Property Protege at the end of the book.

Now, let's head into the final chapters, and bring it all home.

CHAPTER 11:
MOVING FORWARD: THE WAR PLAN

Ok. Would you like the shortcut now? How about the magic button? I know you want to get there fast. But, suffice to say, shortcuts don't exist. I said it before and I'll say it again. When your focus is *get rich quick*. It's most likely you *won't* get rich. But when your focus is fixed on building something to last, with patience, over time, then there's a high chance you *could* get rich, whatever *rich* means to you, and it *doesn't* have to take forever.

Whilst there are no shortcuts, there are ways to accelerate the process, particularly in the form of finding those who are further down the path you wish to travel, and learning from them, which is what we do at Property Protege. Notice, however, that accelerating still means travelling the same path, and going through everything you're going to have to go through, but with the added benefits of the right *Mindset*, right *knowledge*, right *strategy*, and right *action*, with the benefits of the experience and learnings of our team, and the rest of the tribe. No shortcuts, but accelerated progress with fewer pitfalls for sure.

I understand why people look for shortcuts.

I understand the appeal when someone says you can become a Millionaire overnight, or achieve financial freedom in 30 days, or develop a 6-pack without working-out in just a few short weeks. It's the seductive lure of instant results. It's also bullshit; and sadly, there are many people who would be happy to sell you such bullshit.

In the pursuit of wealth through the quickest and easiest means possible, people also cheat themselves by not taking appropriate action, and miss out on the experiences that ultimately build them into an unstoppable version of themselves.

You must never attempt to hide from the problems, the challenges, the learnings, or the obstacles, you must embrace them as part of the journey. You must seek to grow.

Any and all truly successful and wealthy people in my world, played the long game and built it gradually. Had appropriate advice, guidance, and support been available, it would have taken less time for sure, but it would still have taken time and effort.

I remember a conversation with one of my early mentors. He said, "I can show you how to get rich quick." I listened intently for the big reveal. "Yes, I can show you how to get rich quick; wealthy beyond your wildest dreams, in 10 years." Hold on. Time out. 10 years? That's what he said right? "Yes Paul, because 10 years is going to pass in a flash. Most people don't have the resilience to go through the trials and tribulations; the obstacles and challenges; the general shit you're going to have to deal with. 10 years will pass. It'll happen fast, but who will you have become and what will you have achieved?"

Not as motivational as being sold the dream, right?

You came to this book to learn what it takes to build Wealth in Property, and I'm telling you that it's going to take time, and that most will bow out long before they've ever given themselves the chance. That's the real world ladies and gents. But it's not bad news. Quite the opposite; because, whilst many others, who *lack the fortitude, the right mental stuff, the right knowledge, the right strategies, and a consistent commitment to doing the work* fall off the bandwagon and call it a day, you'll have continued to put one foot in front of the other, each and every day, and you will ultimately arrive at your target destination.

I should clarify, for those who have the *eyes to see* and the *ears to hear* what I'm saying, and who've been smart enough to continue to this point; when I'm using the word 'rich,' I'm referring to generational wealth. I'm not talking about a few hundred thousand or a few Million in the bank. I'm talking about creating wealth that lasts for generations. Sadly, most people can't see past next week, let alone 5, 10, and 20 years in the future.

Through Property, when you play the game in the manner I'm suggesting, you absolutely will be able to put yourself in a position to experience wins in a shorter timeframe, providing you do what's required of course; through trading deals, joint ventures, flips, and so on. You could generate a respectable passive income or series of financial windfalls in a relatively short time; but to build serious lifelong and generational wealth, it's going to take time, it's going to take effort, and sadly, it's not going to happen for most people. Not because it's not possible, but because they will simply not do what's required.

PROGRESS AND EXPANSION

I had a chat recently with someone I'd met in 2009. We both started in Property around the same time, but it turns out we've both had very different results. *"You're a lucky man, Paul,"* he said. I wanted to erupt, but kept my cool. He'd been following me online. He seen the house, the cars, the lifestyle, the freedom, the travel, and all the rest of it; which is what most people see. But what he, and others, have not been able to see, is the commitment, the endless days, the obstacles, the challenges, the attacks, the abuse, the sacrifices, the risks, the failures, the lessons learned, the blood, sweat, and tears. Everyone sees the end result, but very few people know what it took and what I had to go through to get there.

I built something. He didn't.

But here's the thing. I'm no better or smarter than him, or anyone else. Less so, likely. But every time they stopped, I took another step. Every time they doubted, I took another step. Every time they put it off, I took another step. Every time they mocked me, I took another step. Every time they played the victim, I took another step. Every hour they spent on social media, I took another step. And every day I woke up, I decided to get after it, no matter what. I was ruthlessly committed to what I was doing. I'm no better than anyone else, I just did the work, and will continue to progress and expand, each and every day.

EXPANDED VISION AND ACCELERATED LEARNING

Earlier in this book, I suggested that most of the roadblocks people when starting or accelerating in Property, are nothing more than mental constructs. Hopefully at this point, you've started to knock down doors that were previously locked, by realising that this is in fact possible for you, despite the odds apparently stacked against you.

The reason that various weights have started to lift, and new doors of possibility have started to open, is because new information changes what we see. More to the point, new information, when properly consumed and understood, changes what we see.

You're on one side of the door. You must get to the other side. Before you can knock, you must be willing to let go of old beliefs, ways of thinking, and ways of being. When you open your mind to new possibilities, and expand your mind through strategic learning, you give yourself the opportunity to knock the door down entirely. But what's on the other side? Another door. Another level of growth. Another element of progress and expansion.

The version of you that takes home £25,000 per annum, is very different from the version of you that takes home £250,000 per annum. You're still you, but much has changed. You've learned. You've grown. You've evolved. And you've reaped the rewards. But notice, it's always internal before its external. Your income can only grow to the extent that you do, and through this book, that process has begun.

I'd like to challenge you here.

At Property Protege and other events we run, whilst sharing content, we have an intense focus on deep and strategic learning. Rather than spraying a fire hose of information into the room, we use various ways and means including breakout sessions, group shares, role plays and more, to ensure that everyone is in alignment, and that people are understanding what's being covered. Through adequate understanding, we can then progress.

So as you read this book, my challenge to you, is to do your own deep dive on *this* content. If you didn't like the book, I doubt you'd still be reading, but please feel free to burn it or throw it away. However, if you found it valuable, I want to encourage you to re-read this content, and in doing so, create an active study. Underline content. Pull out the highlighters. Draw and take notes on the pages. Don't just sit down and read. Take the time to digest various insights. Study a chapter a day. Continually refer back to it. Journal your thoughts.

By doing some, or all, or a variation on the above, you'll find new insights and revelations open up, each time you lean in. The words in this book were not thrown together. They are the cumulation of many years of experience. Right now, based on where you are and who you are, you're taking a specific message from this book. As you grow and expand, you'll take an entirely new meaning from what's covered here. Make this book your companion. Continually refer back to it, and I promise you, the possibilities are endless.

Similarly, when learning other content elsewhere, perhaps at Property Protege, or perhaps in another area of your life, be sure to go deep on what you're learning, and focus intently on strategically studying the content. I want your business. I want you to come and learn with us, and grow with us, and succeed with us, and to be part of the Tribe, but whether you choose to work with us or another, I'd like to strongly recommend that you keep your focus in one place. When you find teachers, mentors, coaches or sources of information or inspiration in any area, and you know that they've walked the walk and are sharing valuable, practical, and useable content, avoid putting your focus elsewhere. Go deep. Consume. Understand. Take action. When you're winning, only then, focus elsewhere.

MOVING FORWARD

Imagine Richard Branson took your place for the next 12-months. Not only would he take your place, but he'd take on your appearance, and would have the exact same tools, resources, and network that you have to work with right now. Do you think that Sir Richard might achieve different results than you would in the year to come? We both know the answer. We also know why. Even if you put Sir Richard on an alternate planet Earth with nothing but his mind, body, and the clothes on his back, he'd still find a way to win.

The good news is, that starting today, you can begin to develop your own Millionaire Mindset. You can choose a different path. You can choose to make better choices. You can choose to expand your vision. You can choose to strategically study. You can choose to die and be reborn again over and over as a continually evolving version of yourself. You can build a bulletproof mind. You can get educated. You can learn the game. And you can win.

No one is stopping you.

Nothing is in your way.

If you don't like where you are, move. You are not a tree.

Since you started reading, nothing has changed, and yet EVERYTHING is different. No more excuses. No more reasons. Time is not a problem. Global pandemics are not a problem. The opinions of other people are not a problem. Belief is not a problem. Confidence is not a problem. Finding the money is not a problem. Finding the deals is not a problem. Finding the information and support is not a problem. There may be challenges, but they are challenges that can be easily overcome; first internally, and then, externally.

No matter your past, you have a spotless future.

If a thing is humanly possible, it is within your reach.

Wake up.

It's your turn now.

PROPERTY SUCCESS MINDSET

CHAPTER 12:
NEXT STEPS: PROPERTY PROTEGE ®

In January 2010, after being active in Property for several years, having gone through many of the experiences you've read about in this book, I set up one of the UK's largest Property Networking events, across two cities. I was 24 years old but looked about 12.

I set up the event for a number of reasons. I wanted to expand my network. I thought it would be fun. I saw the limited number of similar events, and I believed I could do it better. I wanted to create a resource that didn't exist in the way I felt it *could* and *should*; a resource that I wished had been available to me, in the preceding years.

As the events took off, and began to grow from strength to strength, a number of people began asking if I'd be willing to teach what I'd learned throughout my journey. They knew I'd invested heavily in my education and had learned from the best and brightest in Property and Business. They knew I'd come from nothing and had been successful at a young age. They also knew that I'd amassed a level of knowledge and experience that was unmatched by a majority of others in the local Property community.

At the time, I couldn't think of any good reason why I'd want to teach others. I was doing well financially, and didn't see sense in sharing that information.

Then one day, a few years later, I began to see things a little differently. After continual ongoing requests for help and support, I began to look at the Property Education space, and noticed four key problems. 1) a lack of experience in many educators. 2) poor quality of information and delivery. 3) a serious lack of support. 4) continual upsells.

I saw a gap in the market, and felt I could do it better. I saw a way that I could work with people to give them the tools and resources to succeed in Property, whilst creating potential future Joint Venture and Business Partners who understood my Mindset and approach, and not be upset if they did deals without me, because they'd paid me for the information. I weighed up the pros and cons, made my decision, and Property Protege was born.

What happened from there was interesting. As someone who made money doing deals, I'd never truly stopped, analysed, and dissected my approach; but now I had to. I began to build a system that other people, from all walks of life, could tap into, to produce results. I had to take into account those with money and those without, those with time and those without, those with connections and those without, those who were in the game and those who simply wanted to be. I had to learn how to teach, mentor and coach, in a way that worked for all involved. I began to build a framework of training and support, which was virtually unmatched in how it operated, and also in terms of the results of our clients.

Those results have continued to pour in to this day, and our ongoing commitment to provide what our clients need, also continues to evolve to this day, to ensure that whilst we have no desire to be the biggest or open our doors to everyone, we are absolutely committed to being the irrefutable best. Not by our own measures, but by the results of the Tribe. When I tell you Property Protege is the best thing since sliced bread, you'd expect it. I'm biased. What you must do, is listen to the wins of our clients. At **PropertyProtege.com** we've featured over 200 videos including case studies over an hour long. Don't take my word for it. Take the word of countless others who've put the system to work.

SO WHAT IS PROPERTY PROTEGE ®?

Property Protege is the programme I wish existed when I first started. If it had, I'd have significantly fast tracked my journey. It wouldn't have taken me years to go full-time. I'd have made more money on my deals. I'd have known where to find those deals. I'd have known how to raise finance. I'd have had more strategies and exits in my toolkit. I'd have navigated through the mistakes and pitfalls with less pain and drama. I'd have been significantly more successful, in a shorter timeframe. And, I'd have been in good company.

When you get started on the Property Protege 12-month programme, there are 6 key things to be aware of, that constitute the programme.

1. Pre-event training. Before you attend the Property Protege event, you will be given access to the pre-event training modules in our Members Only Property Vault. The modules are video based, and walk you through the foundations and fundamentals of Property. This ensures that you understand the game and are fully equipped to make the most of our time together.

2. The Property Protege Live event. This is where we go deep. We'll spend three full days together; starting early and finishing late. You won't just be listening. We'll be learning, we'll be working, we'll role play, we'll push through our comfort zones, and we'll have a lot of fun. At the event we'll cover a myriad of topics, including Mindset, fundamentals, foundations, due diligence, goldmine area research, working the numbers, investment strategies, buy-to-let, buy-to-flip, deal trading, deal structuring, deal sourcing, negotiation, raising finance, finding investors, tax mitigation, joint ventures, and more. We'll also cover advanced strategies including options, delayed completions, first time buyers strategy, assisted sales, and title splitting. After 3 intense days, we'll wrap up the event with your War Plan, and make sure that no question goes unanswered, and that everyone is clear in their learning. It may seem like a lot, however, coupled with the pre-event training, you'll be surprised how far you'll come from the time you start learning, to completing the live event.

3. Post-event content. After the event, we'll open up the Property Vault, and give access to advanced material and our post event modules. You'll have full access to exclusive content covering key subjects including business structures, systemisation, company setup, compliance, and supplementary training to

enhance what you've learned at the live event, ensuring that you can go back, reference the content, and continue learning.

4. Weekly group coaching video calls. Dial in and join others in the Property Protege community; get access to regular additional training and up-to-date content and information, learn what's working in the market at any given point in time, listen as others check-in, sharing their deals and wins, and overcoming challenges with the support of our team and Tribe members, live on the calls, which can go on for hours at a time.

5. Private online support group. Ask a question, and you'll get a response. My team are in there, ready to help and support you, as are the rest of the Tribe. When you go out into the world of Property, that's when the real learning takes place. You'll need help. This group, and the zoom calls, are where it happens. The private support group is also a great community environment where others share regularly, including myself and my team. It's a clean group. It's an immensely valuable resource, and there's zero tolerance for bullshit.

6. The Property Protege Tribe. You'll be joining a phenomenal network, a group where lifelong friendships are made, partnerships are struck, and deals are done. Check your ego at the door, and join a group of like-minded people, at various stages of the journey and with various levels of success and results, from those who are just getting started, to those who have produced Million+ portfolios and wins. I'm proud of the network that's formed around us, and the extent that people go to, to support one another.

There's no reason why anyone cannot be successful through Property Protege, whatever success means to you. Before the event, you have extensive, detailed, and dissected training. During the live event, which is held in either Glasgow or London, we go deep and immerse ourselves in an environment of learning and doing. You then have access to the post-event training, where we give further relevant information, on the legal, compliance, and business aspects of running your Property business. You have the full support of our team and Tribe for 12-months, through the weekly zoom calls, our private support group, and in many occasions in person. Nothing is left out, and everything is given.

HOW DO YOU GET STARTED?

We do not operate like other companies. With Property Protege, you simply cannot go online and pay to attend. You cannot simply buy your way in. You cannot run to the back of the room and find yourself with a discount ending in a seven.

We want to make sure the fit is right. As such, there is an application process. You must speak with a member of my team. We want to ensure that this is the right fit for you. We want to ensure that you're going to get what you're looking for. We want to ensure that you're prepared and ready to do the work. We want to ensure that you have no illusions of magic pills or get-rich-quick fantasies. We also want to make sure that you're the right fit for us, and our Tribe, as you will be part of that Tribe for 12-months, perhaps longer. We are protective over our community, and providing the fit is right, we'd love to have you. Don't worry, we don't bite. We simply want to make sure this is right for you and for us.

I should also mention, I don't just want your business for 12-months. I want you to be part of our Tribe for many years to come. We have Proteges who've been with us for many years. Why? Because they got what they were looking for, they did the work, they tapped into the support, and they recognise the immense value of what we do here.

Whatever your situation, we want to talk to you.

Go to **PropertyProtege.com**, fill in the application form, and schedule your call.

LET'S GET TO WORK

Here's the reality of the situation. I make my money doing deals. My team make money doing deals. My clients make money doing deals. We are a deal-doing-enterprise first, and an education company second. As such, we know exactly what's required to win.

Whilst from time to time we'll offer additional complimentary training, we have no interest in pushing continual up-sells on you. Everything you want from Property Protege, everything it is, you'll receive, and you will be armed with the Mindset, education, resources, strategies and support, to generate cash flow, and build wealth through Property.

I want you to win. I want you to succeed. I want to work with you for years to come and to get to know you. I can't speak for other training companies, but I can speak for my own, when I say that everything you may have hoped for is available to help you get started, it's available right now, and it's waiting for you at Property Protege. Remember, don't just listen to me. Go to PropertyProtege.com and watch and listen to the hundreds of case studies and testimonials from others who've gone through the Programme.

It's time to wrap up for now.

I don't imagine you'd have read this additional section of the book if you didn't have an interest in continuing the conversation with us. If that is the case, I look forward to meeting you, and to making big things happen with you in Property.

If you've finished here and choose to travel the road on your own, I want to tell you that I respect you immensely for making it this far in the book, and wish you nothing but luck on the journey. I hope to meet you one day too, and to hear your story.

Thanks for reading.

Drop me a review on Amazon if you enjoyed it.

And drop in on social and say hello.

Speak soon. Paul.

PROPERTY PROTEGE ®

To learn more about Property Protege ® and to hear from many of the people who have already attended, go to:

propertyprotege.com

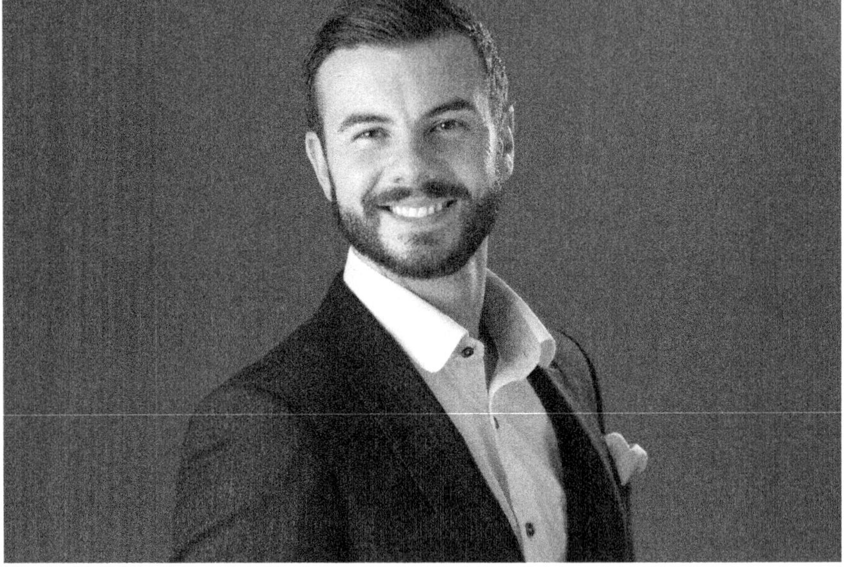

ABOUT THE AUTHOR

Paul McFadden is a renowned and respected high performance, property, and business success coach. As a successful entrepreneur and authority on wealth creation, Paul's ongoing mission and commitment is in supporting others in developing their own wealth through property and business.

After a difficult start in life, growing up in a single parent household with little to no financial resources, Paul discovered that a lack of resources was less important than an attitude of resourcefulness, coupled with a strong mindset of possibility and good old hard work.

From a standing start, with no personal funds, no experience, and no track record, Paul built a multi-million pound portfolio, has bought and flipped millions of pounds worth of Property, and has packaged and traded tens of millions of pounds worth of Property deals to other investors, as well as being responsible for helping countless others (including many prominent well-known professionals in the industry) go full-time in Property.

Whether through Paul's free resources online, or by helping you transform your fortunes in property and business through training, mentoring and coaching, Paul hopes to help you live a full expression of yourself, and discover your own power and capabilities.

paulmcfaddenwealth.com

Printed in Great Britain
by Amazon